Capturing Beauty

By Andy Keith

Text Photo Copyright c 2019 Andy Keith

William Penrose Publishing

All Rights Reserved

To Suzy, Kayla, Chloe, Mary, Tyler, Emma and Tucker

Published in Loving Memory of

Karen Keith and Carol Keith McWilliams

Preface

This little book of pictures is my feeble attempt at capturing beauty. A few years ago I was very sick. When I got better and started waking from sleep and not from the dead I noticed there was beauty everywhere. I have taken thousands of pictures this year alone. These pictures are a sampling of the last several years and I hope you enjoy them.

My sister Carol was a real photographer and I remember always wishing I could do what she did. Since she's been gone I like to think I see things the way she must have seen them. My sister Karen was a pianist and in her short life made beautiful music. My sisters have left me a legacy of capturing beauty and appreciating all that each day brings.

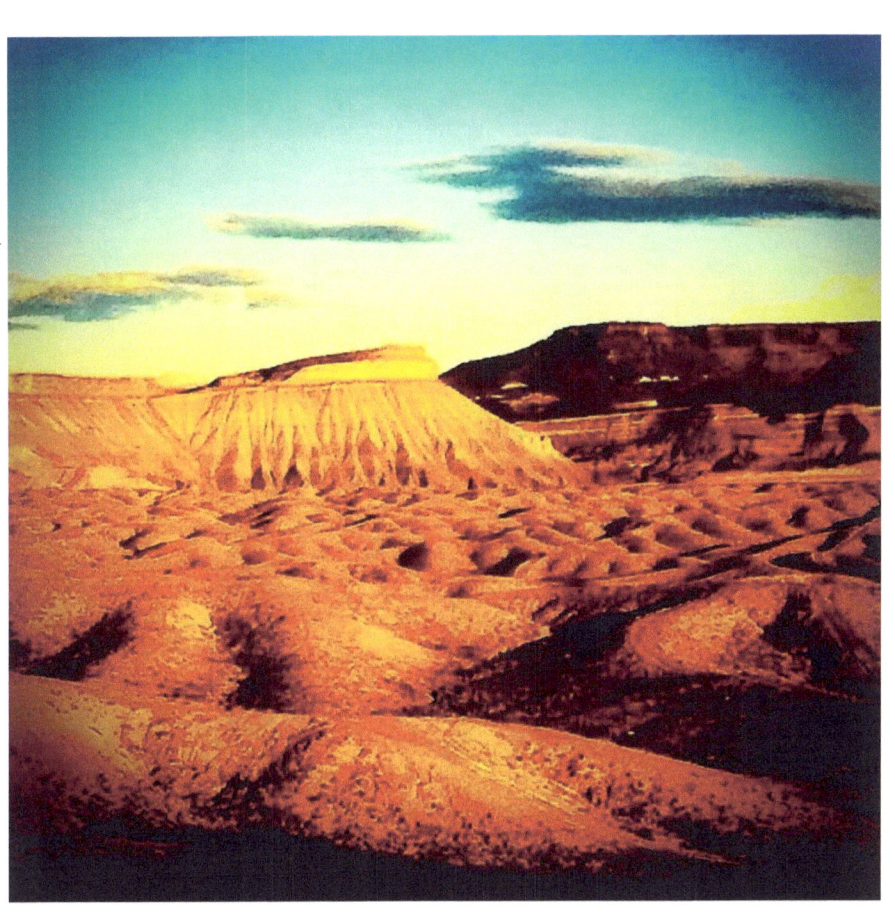

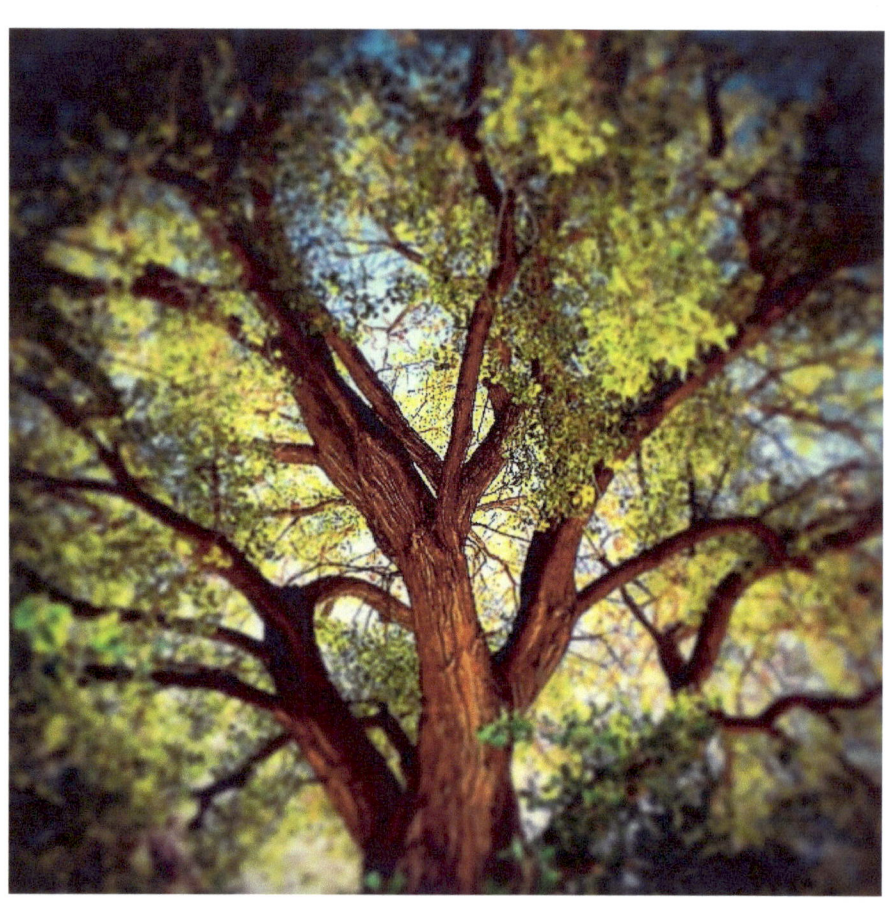

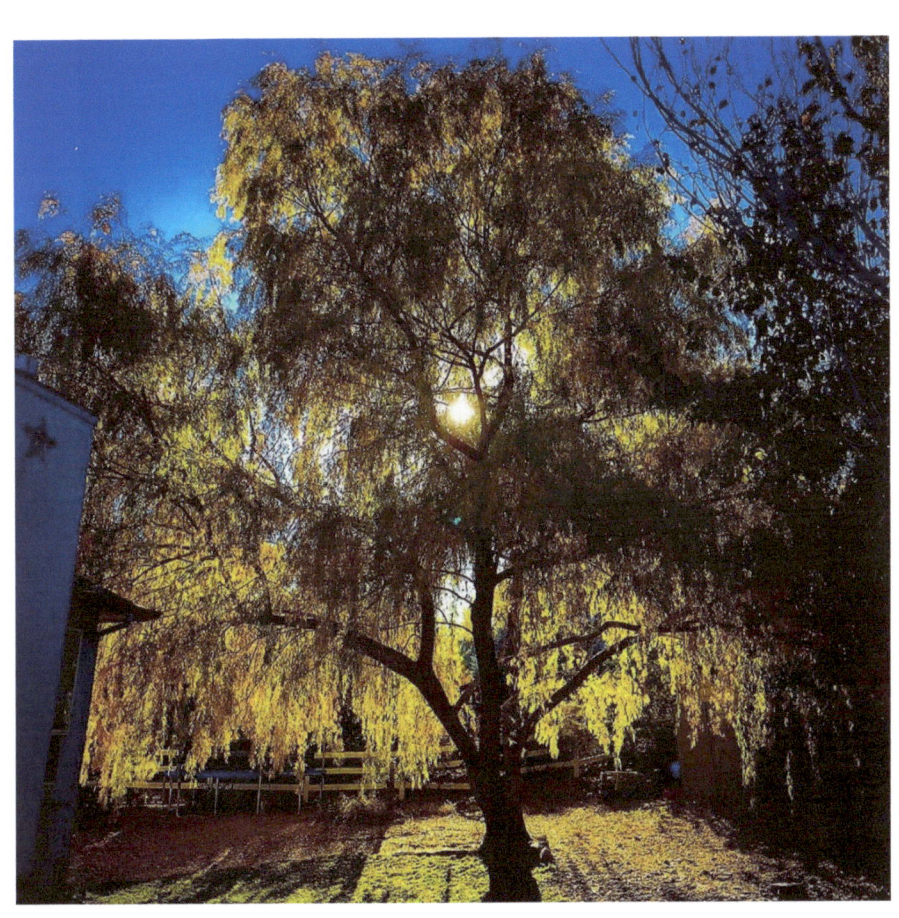

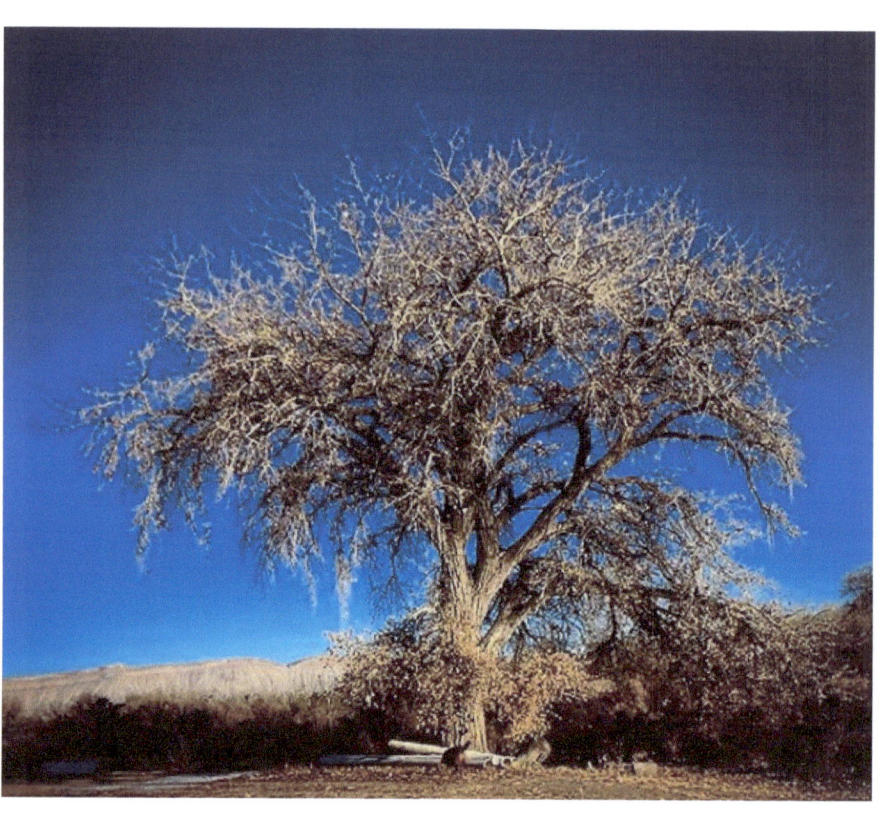

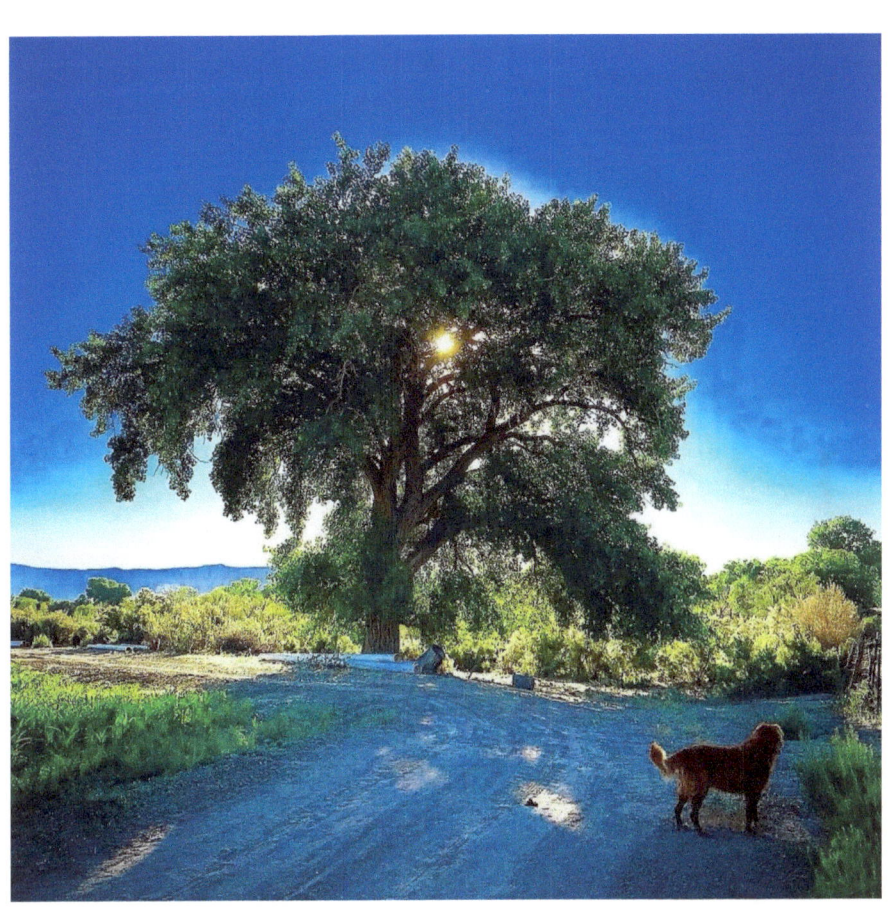

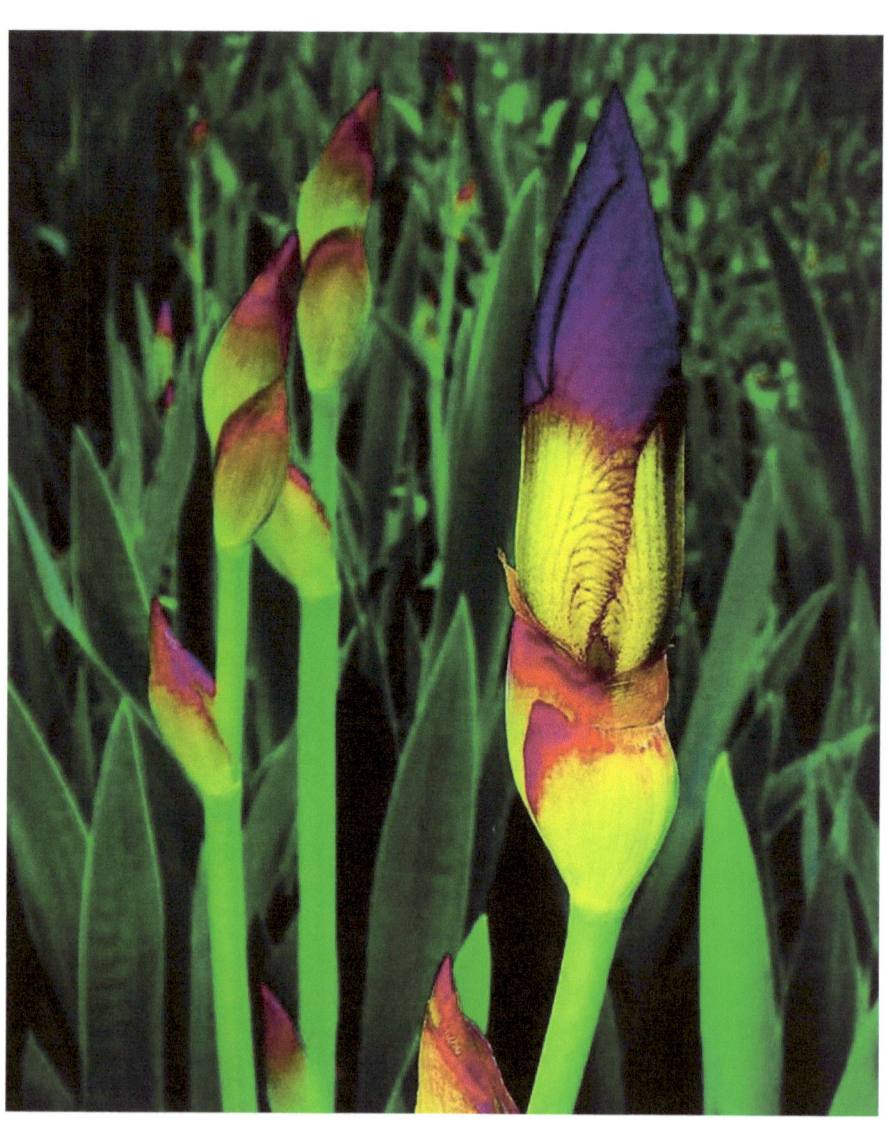

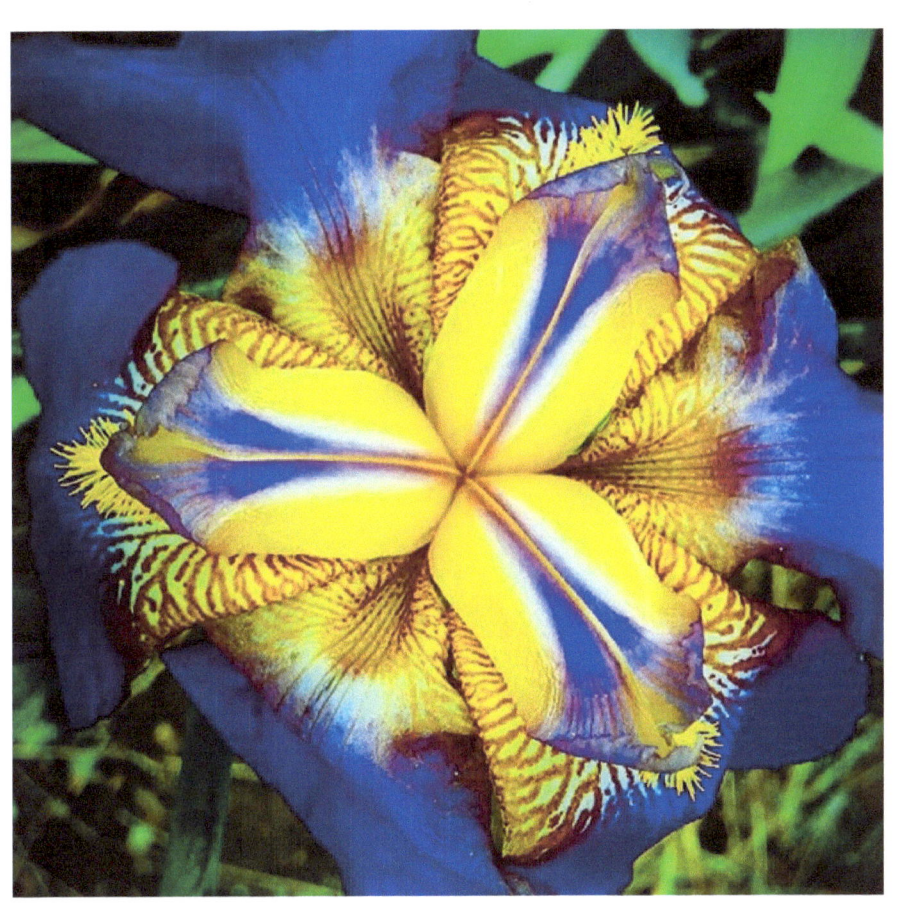

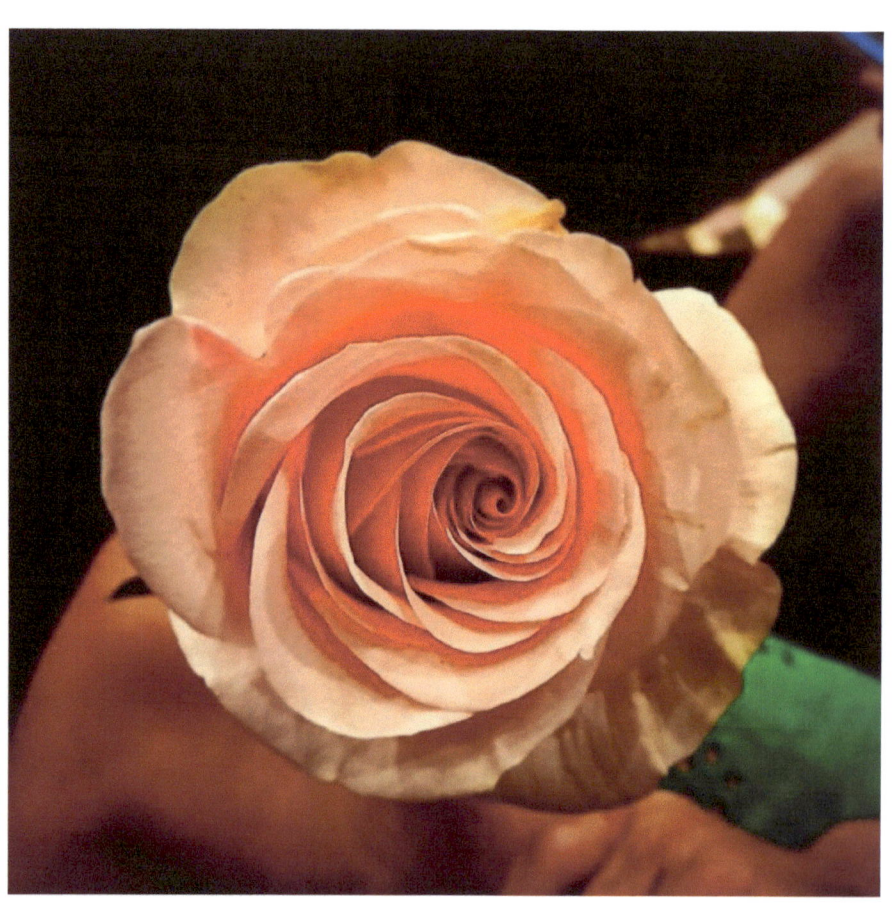

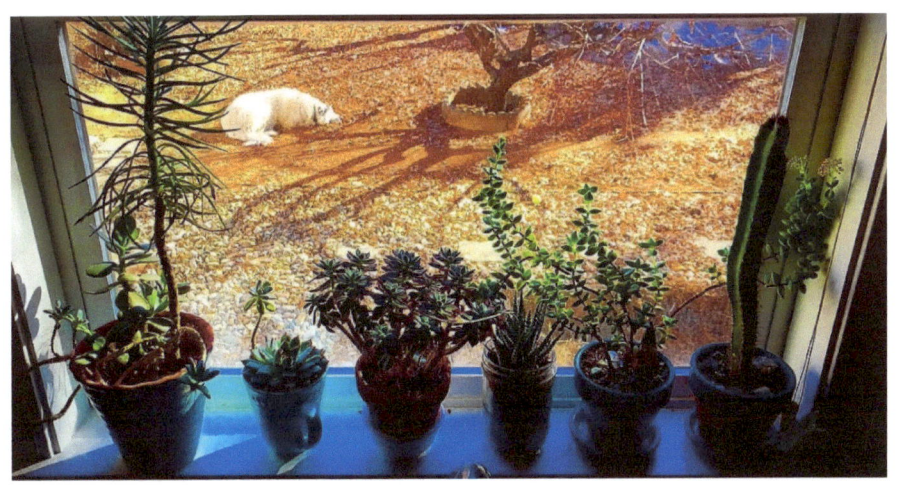
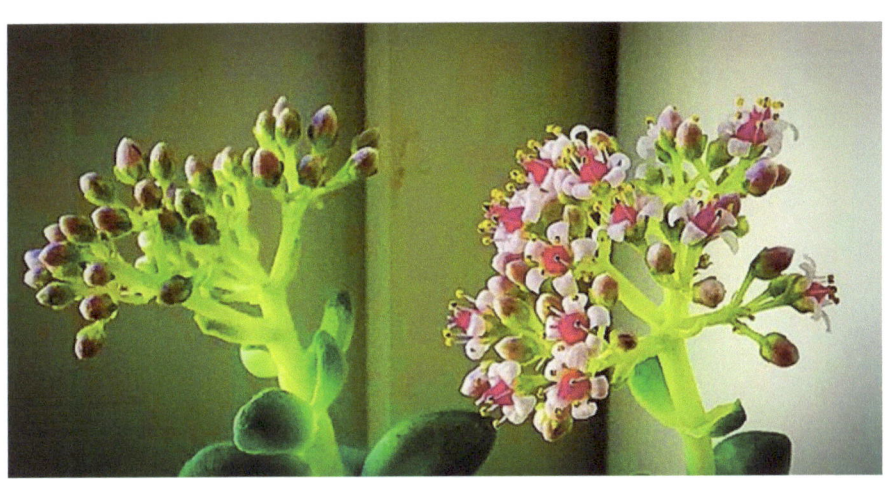

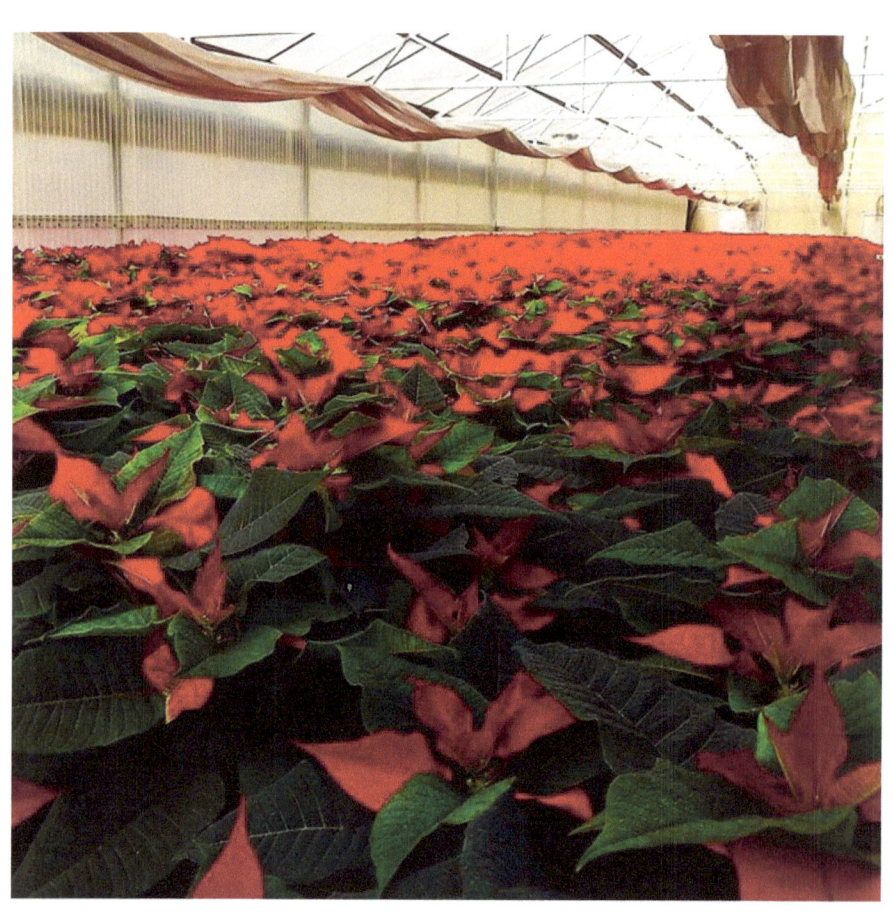

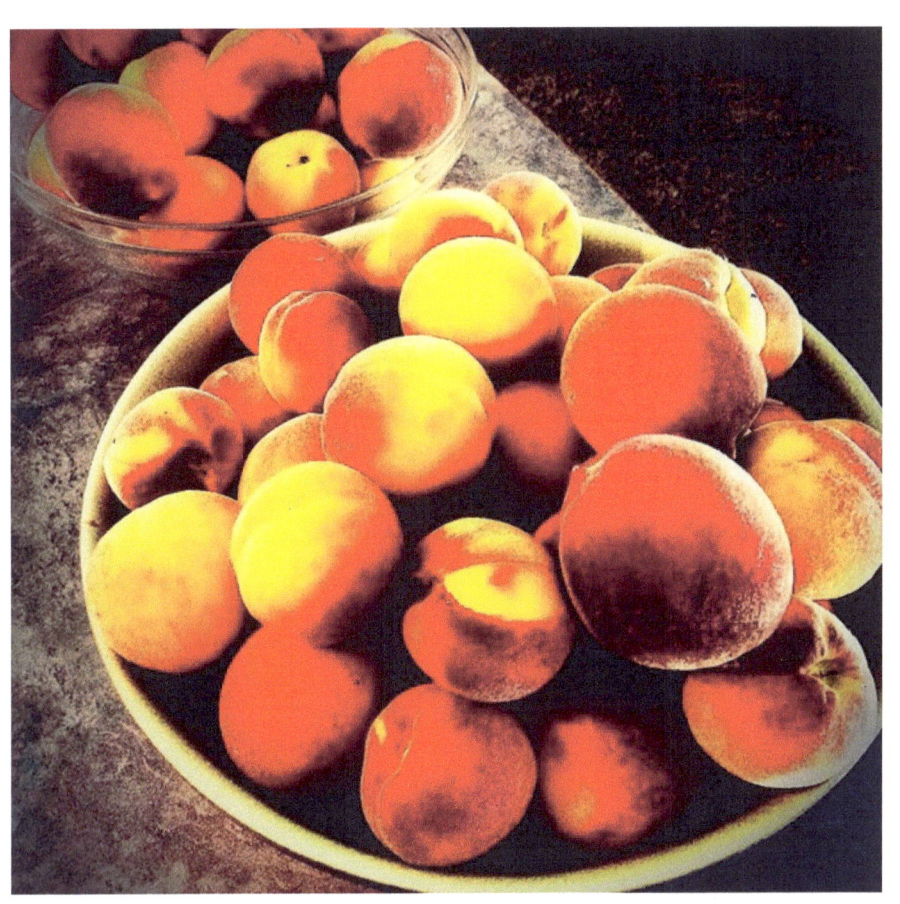

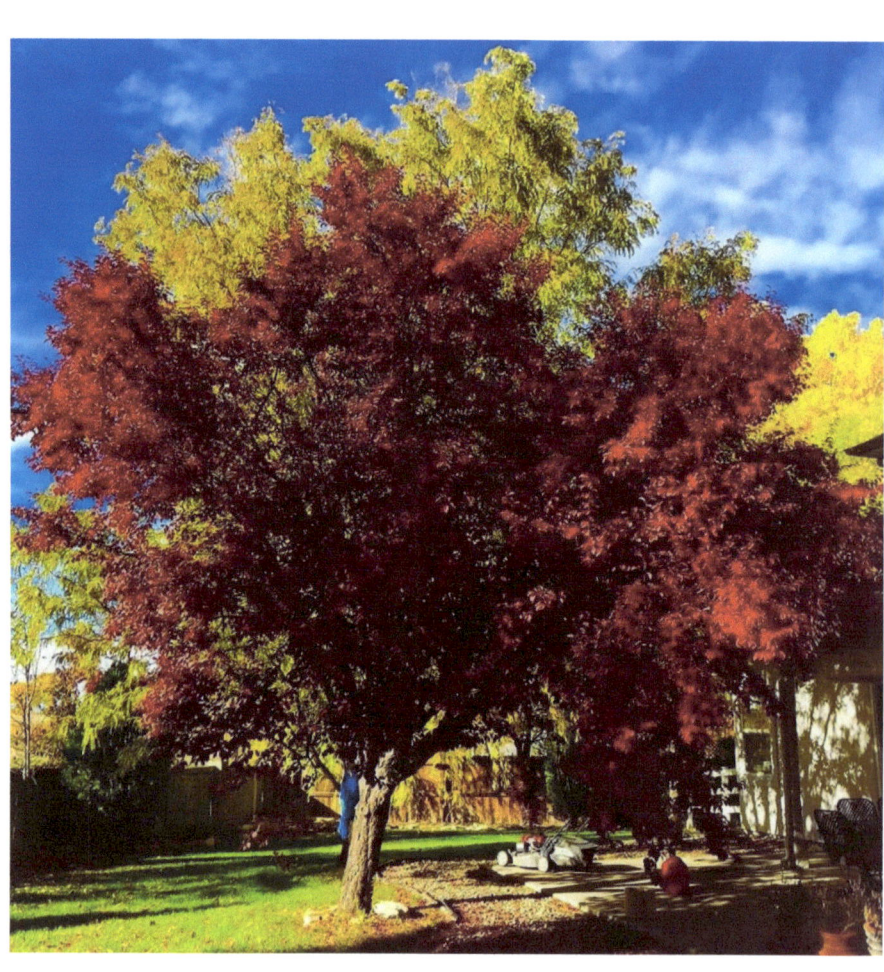

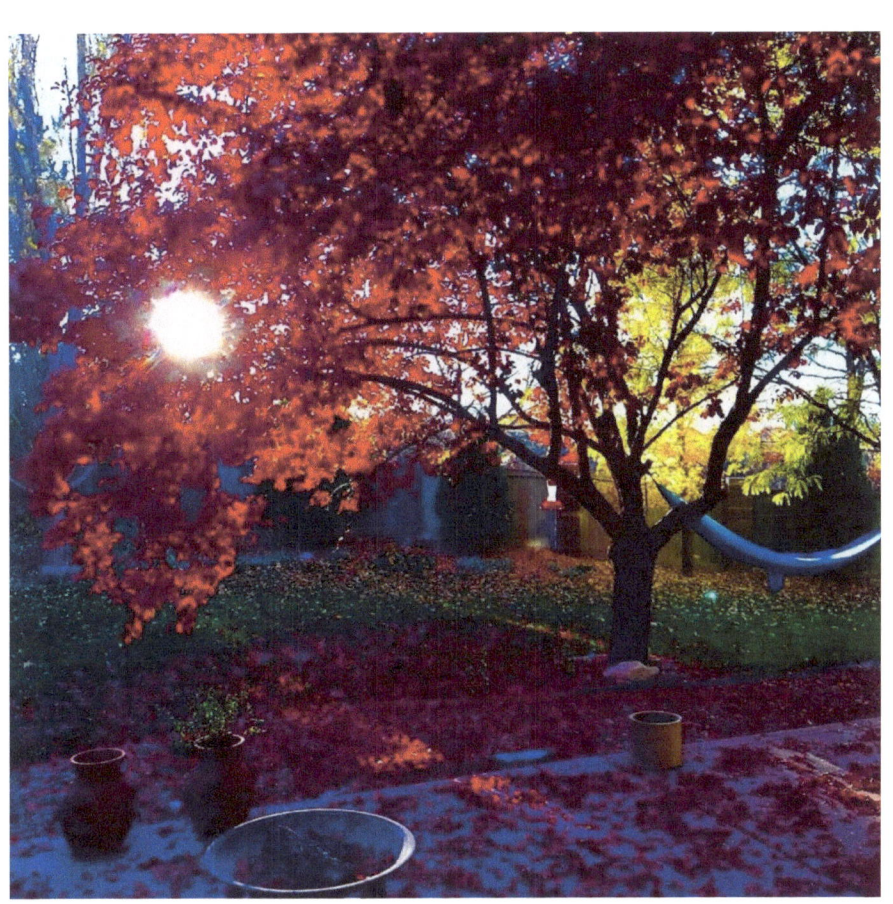

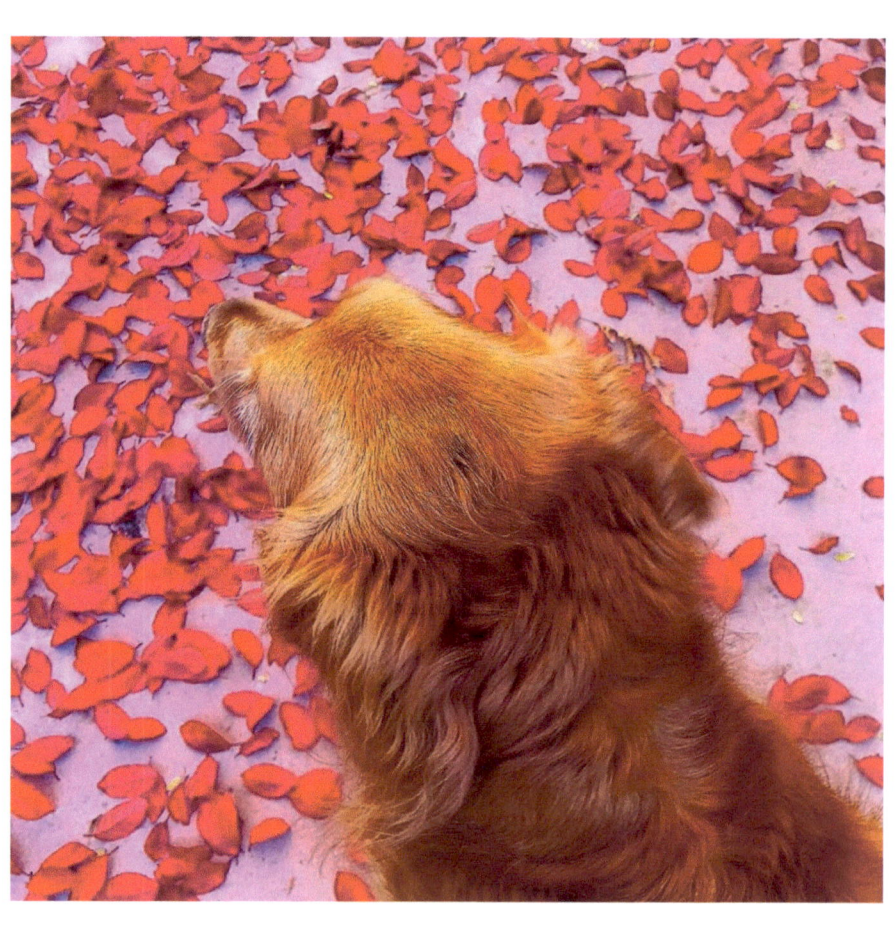

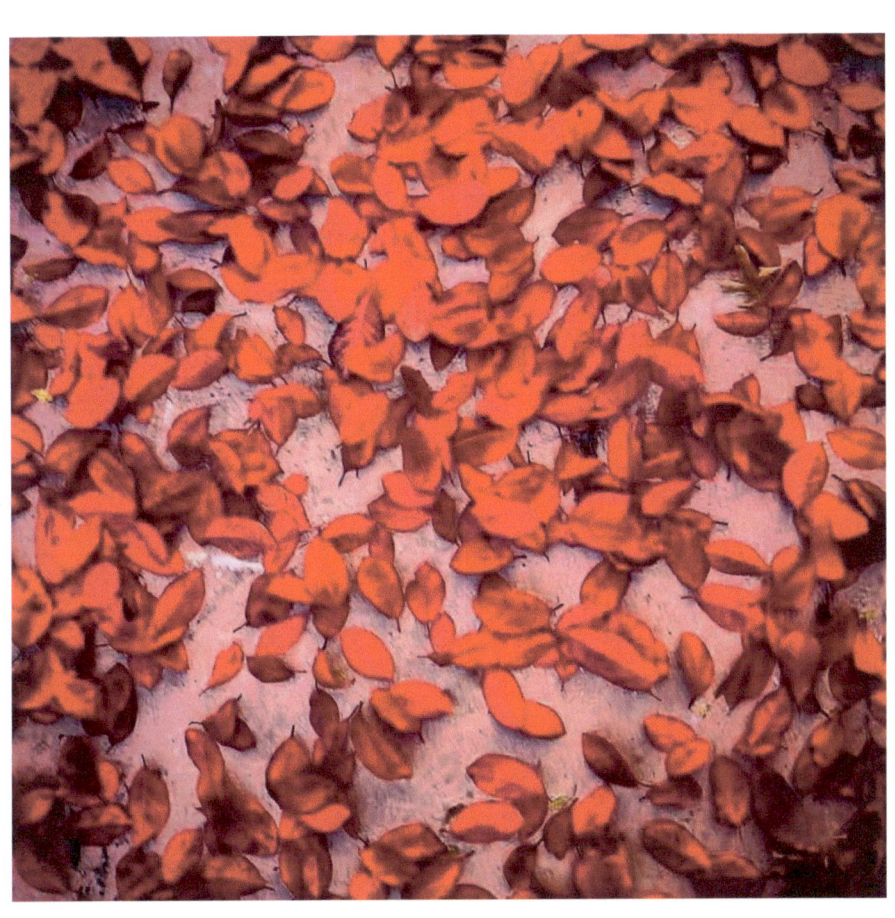

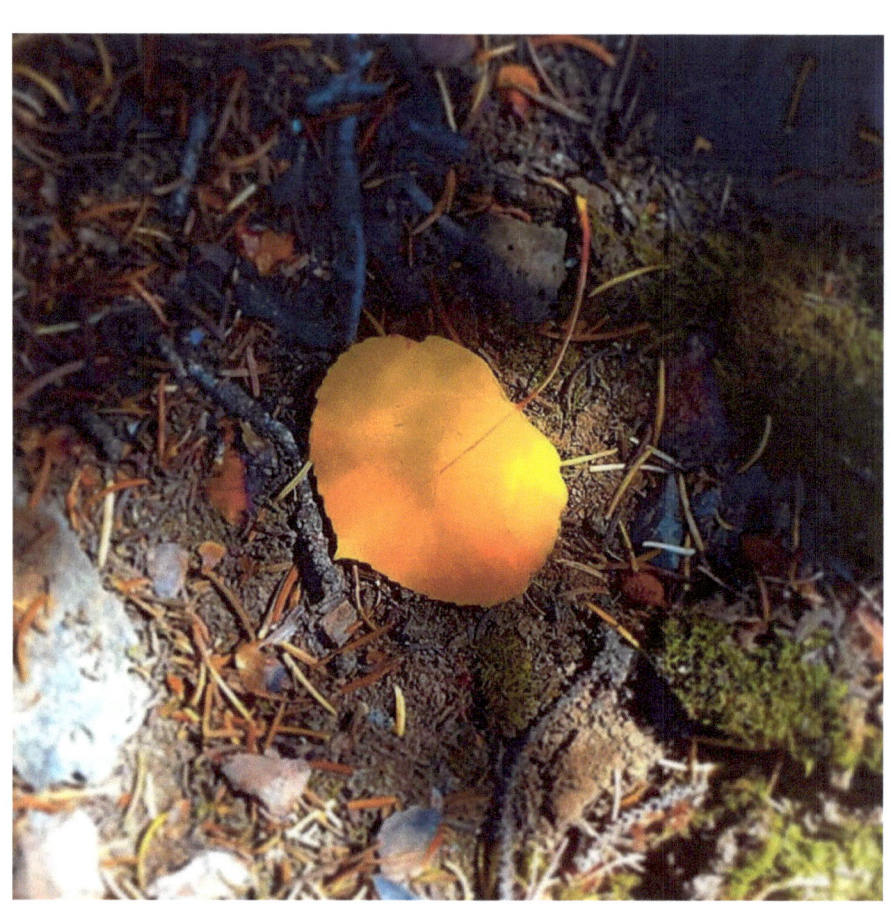

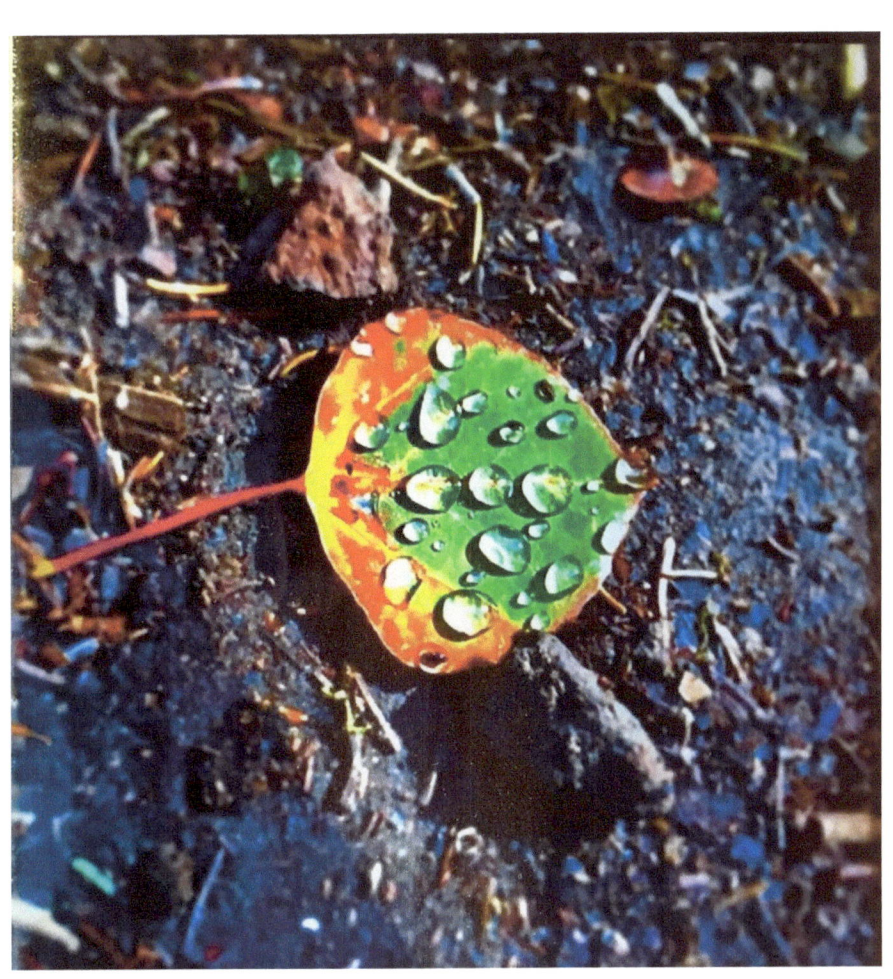

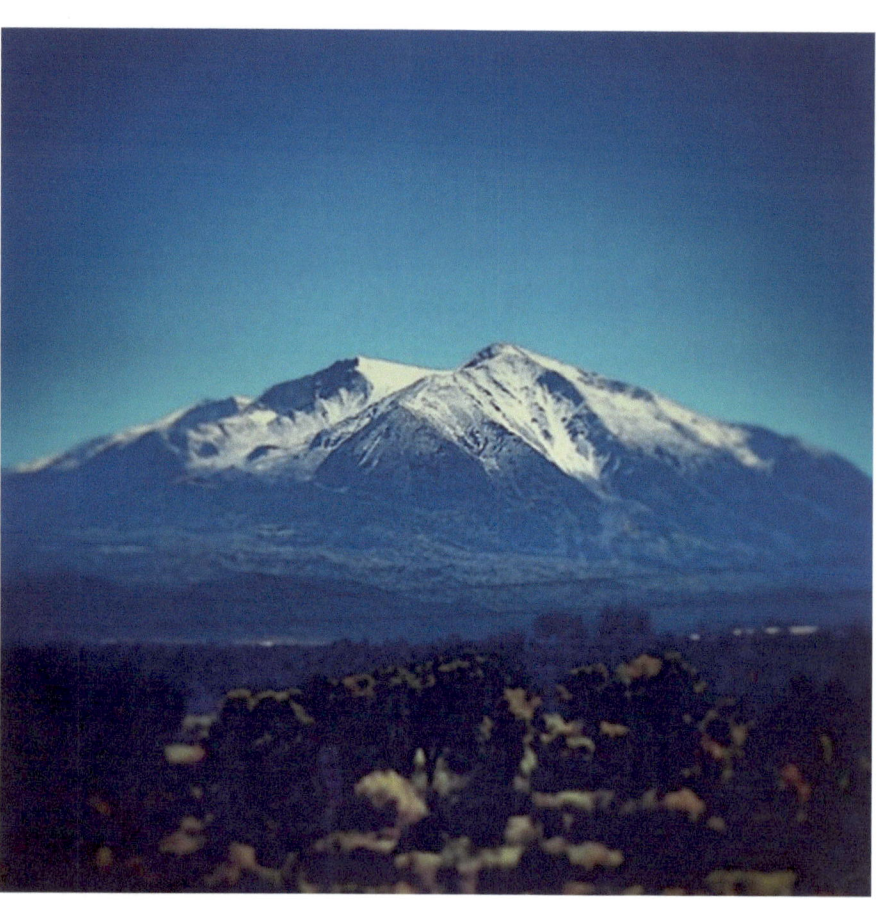

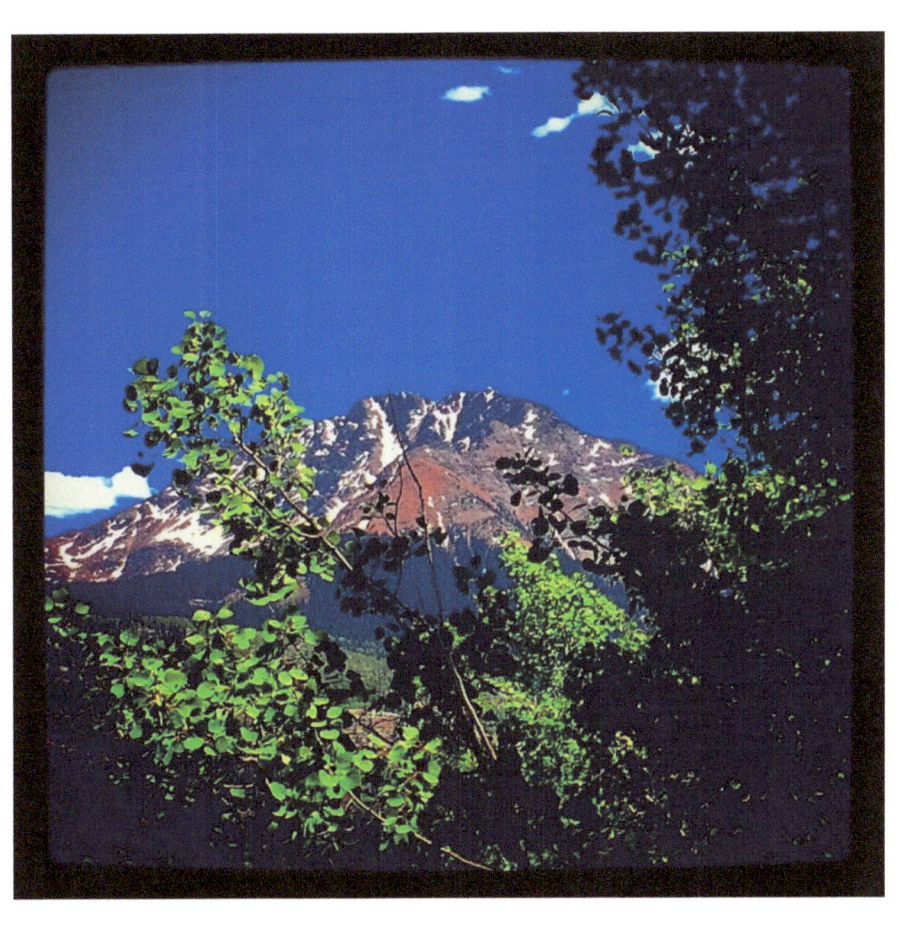

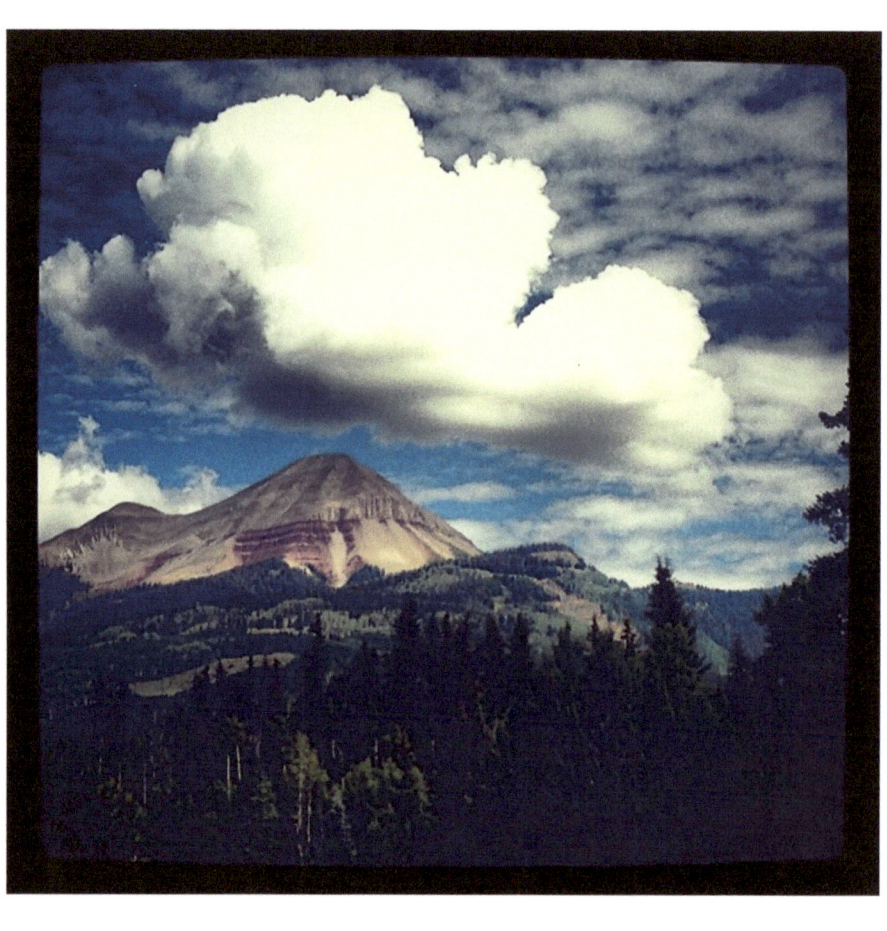

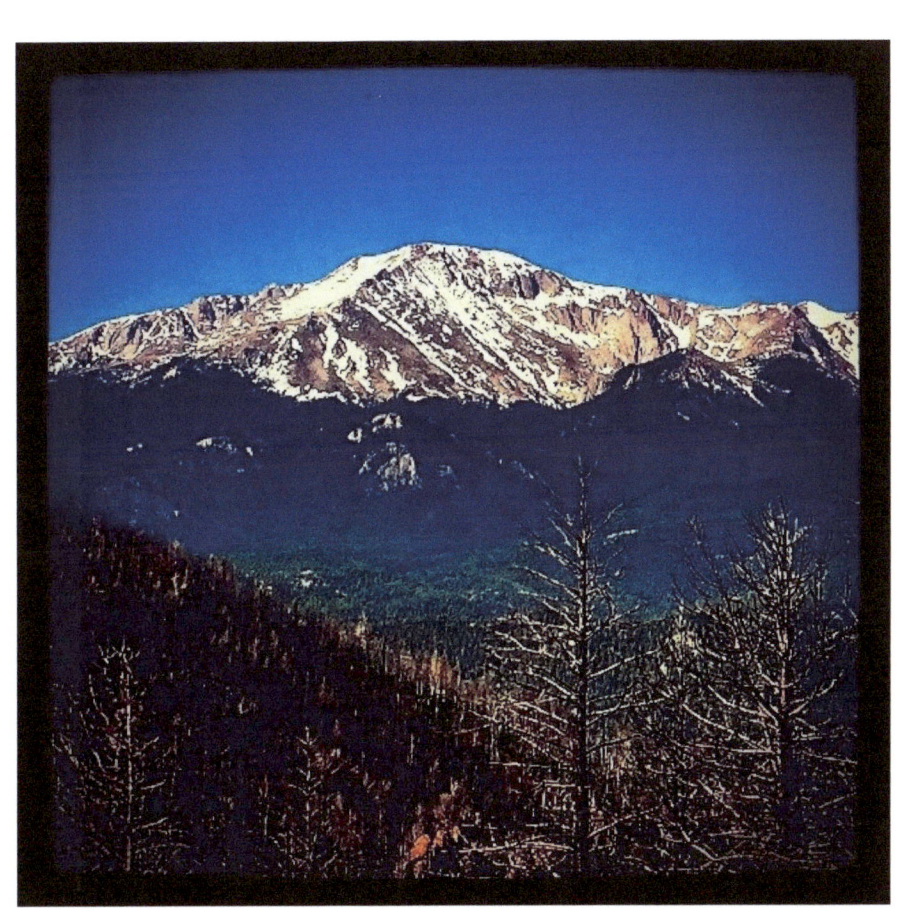

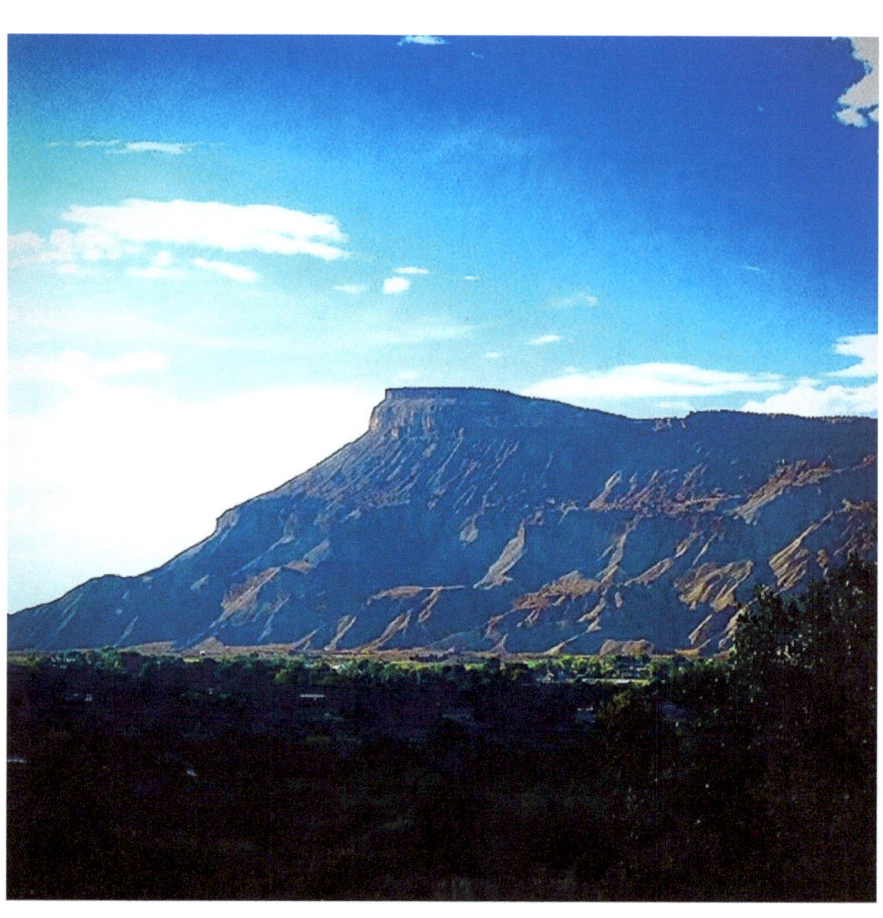

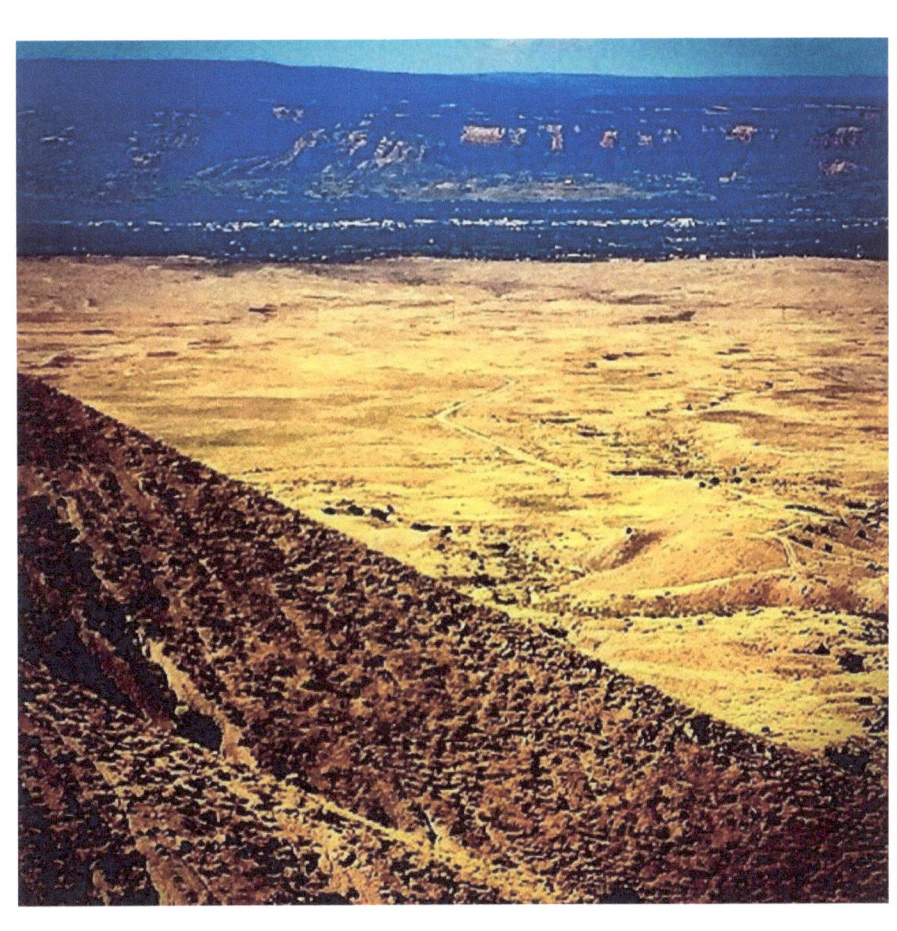

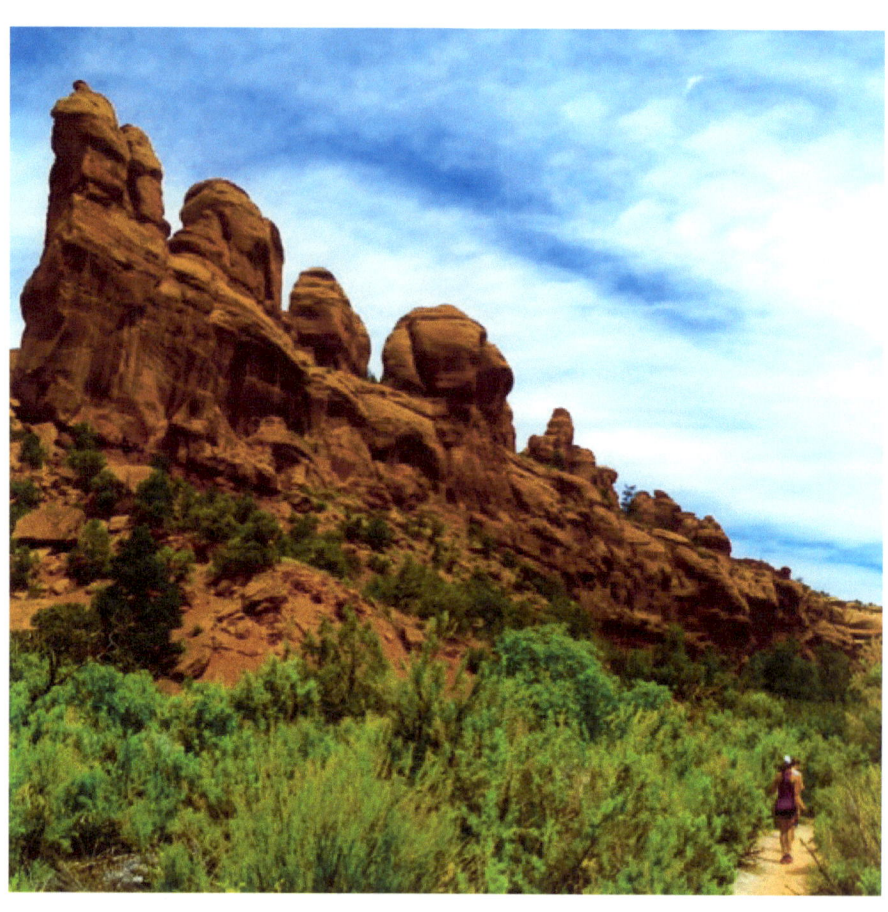

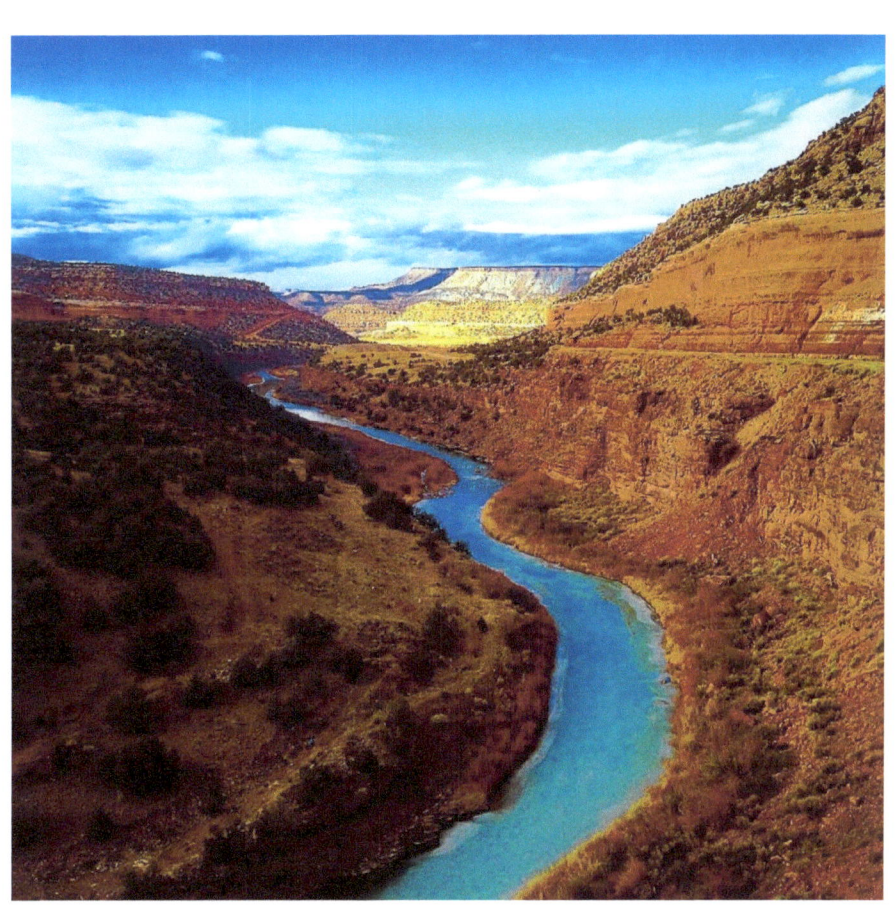

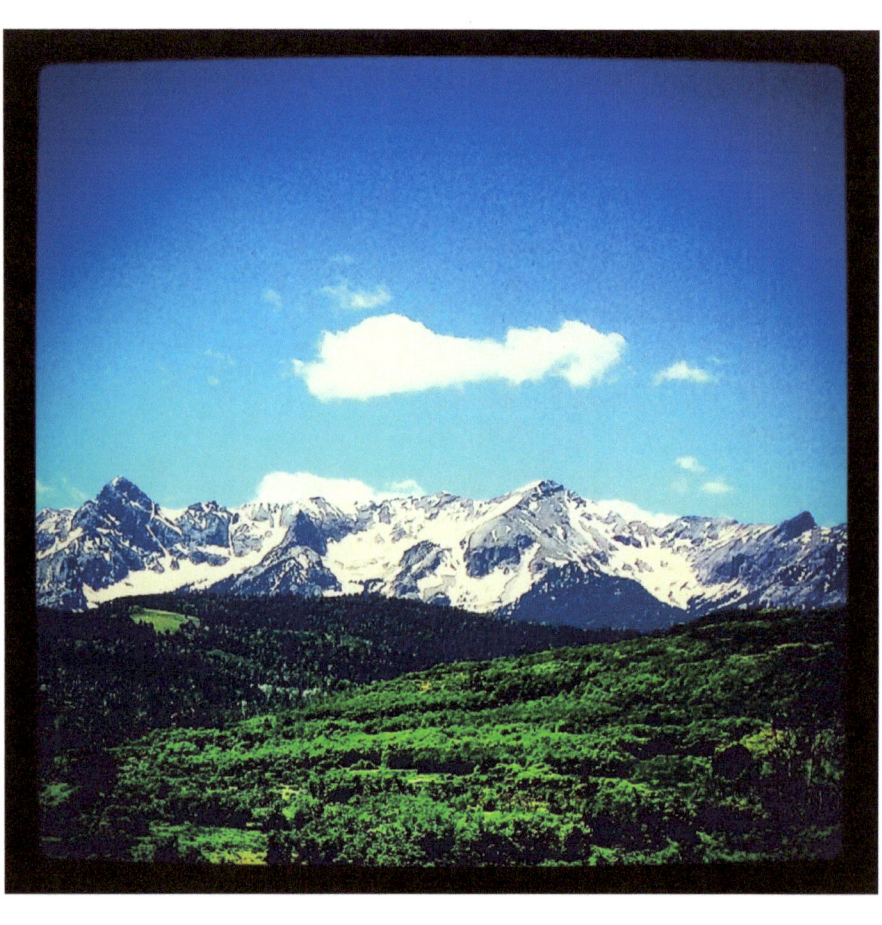

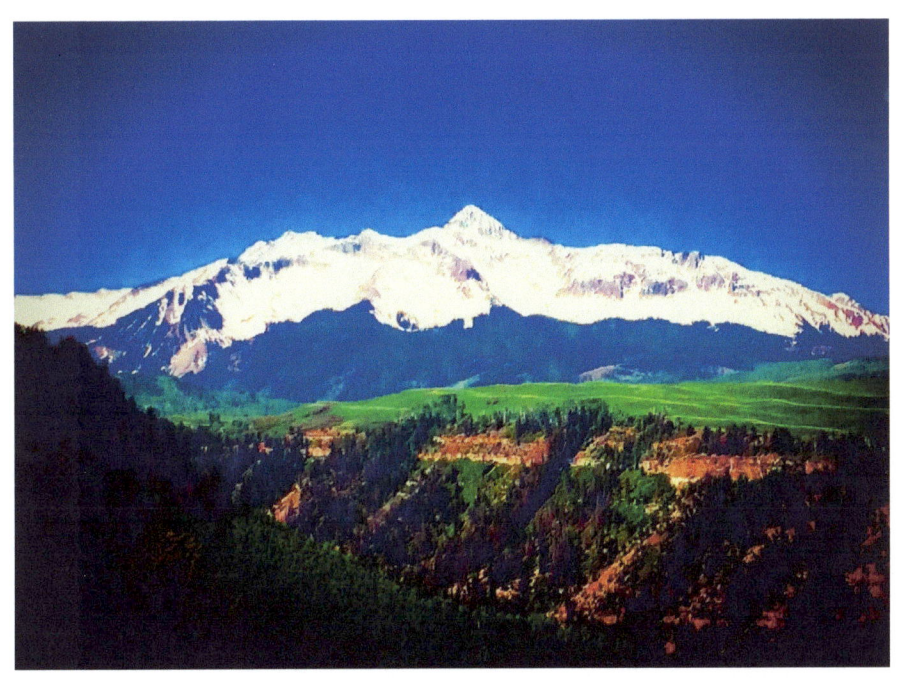

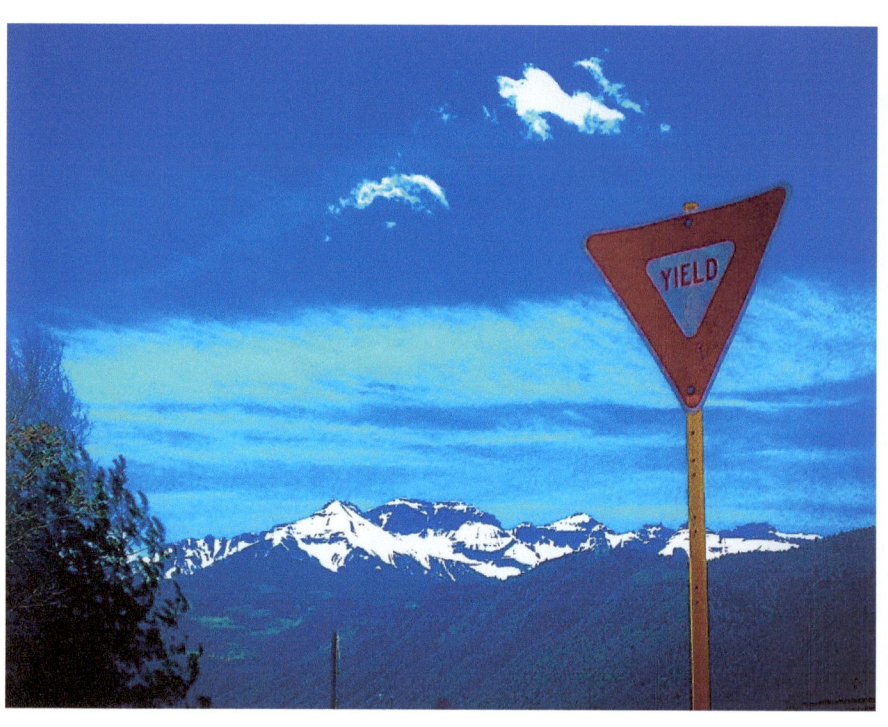

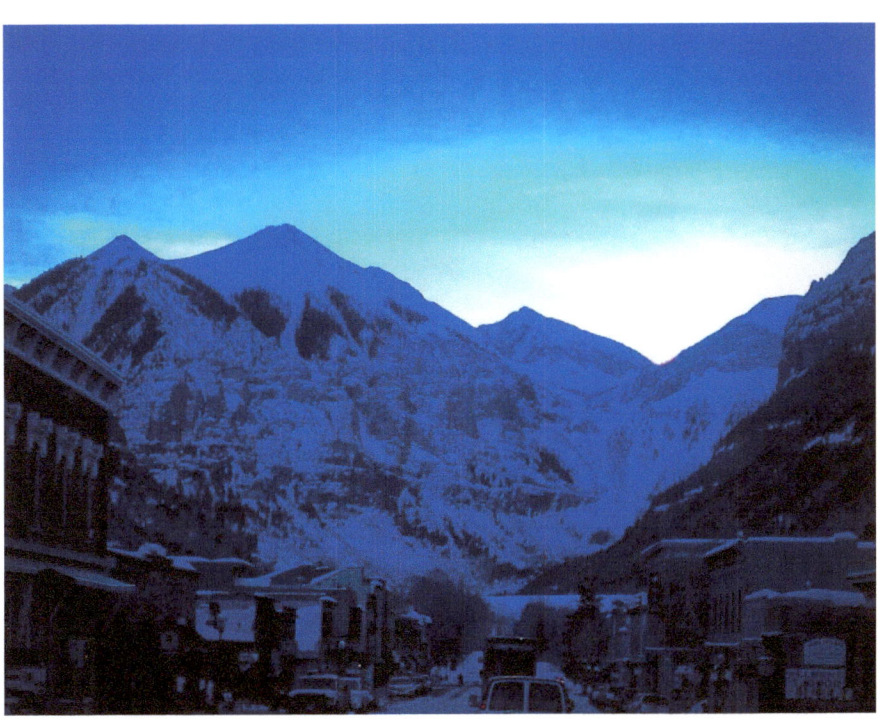

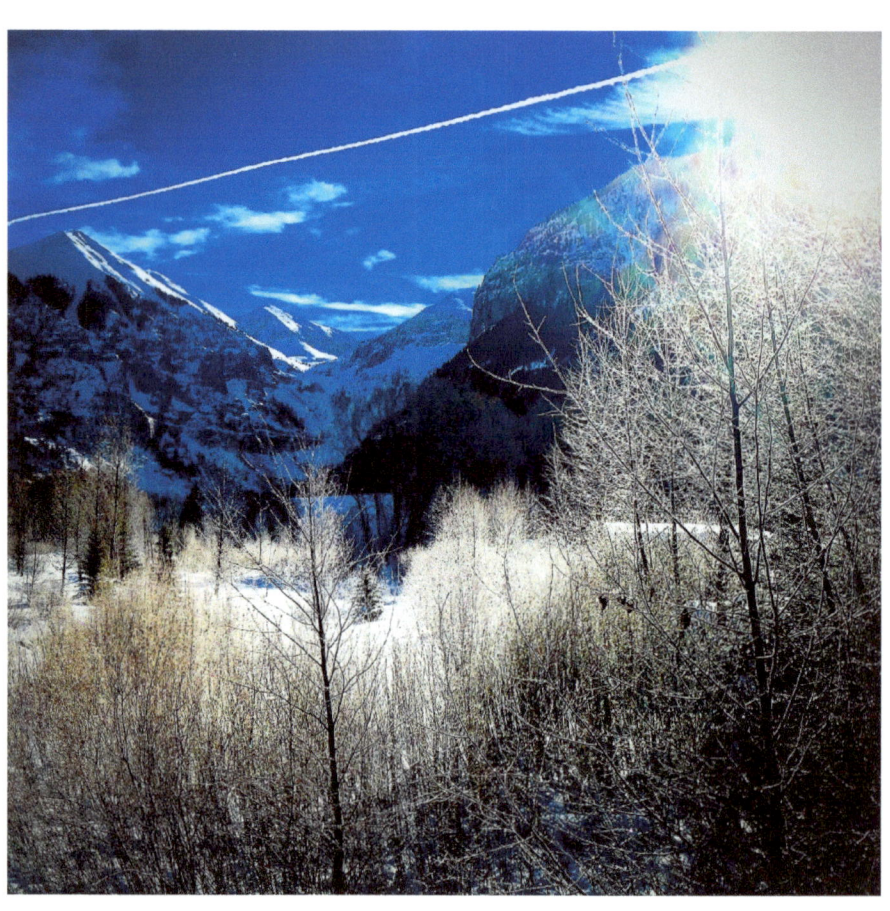

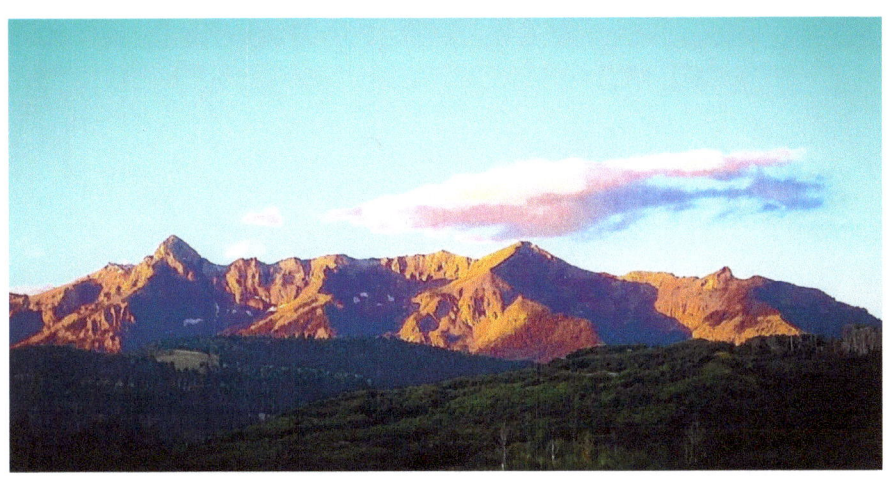

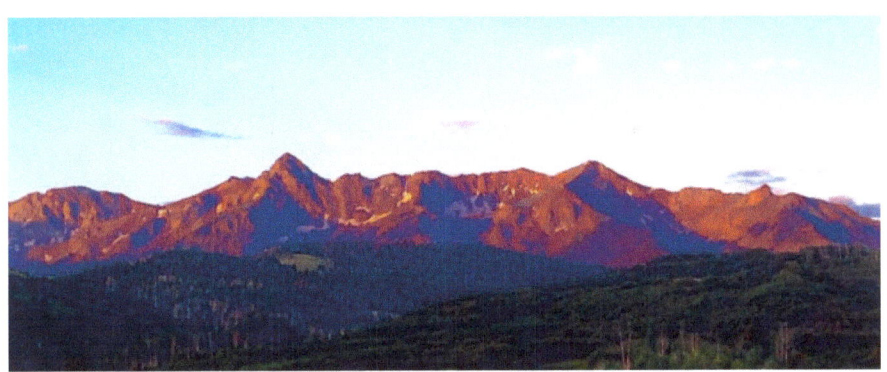

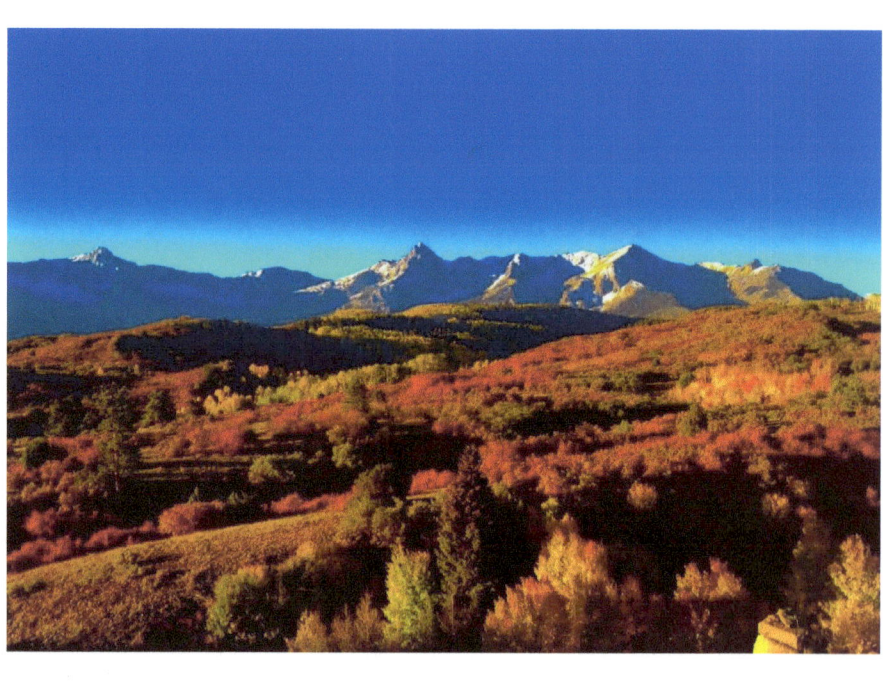

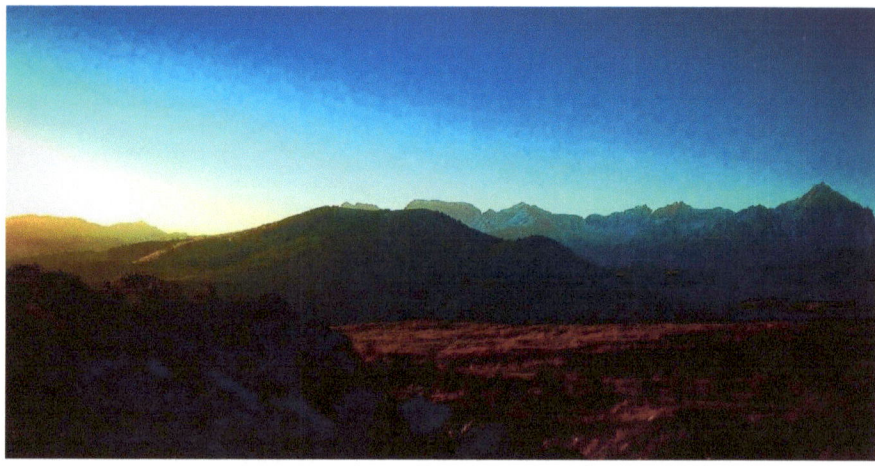

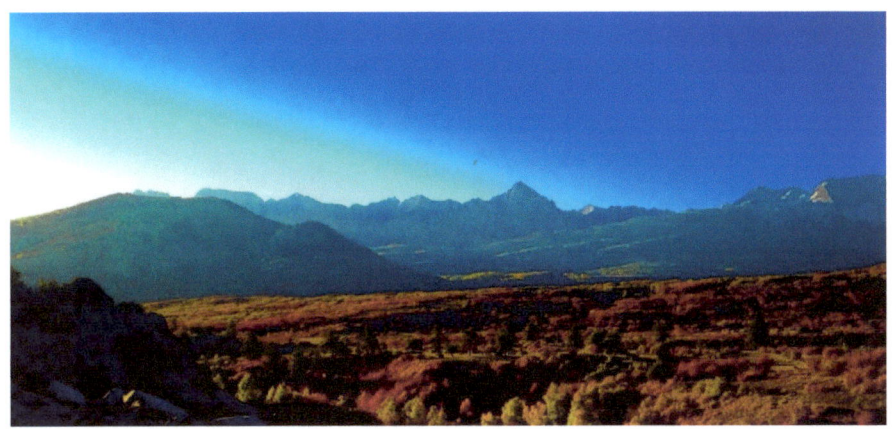

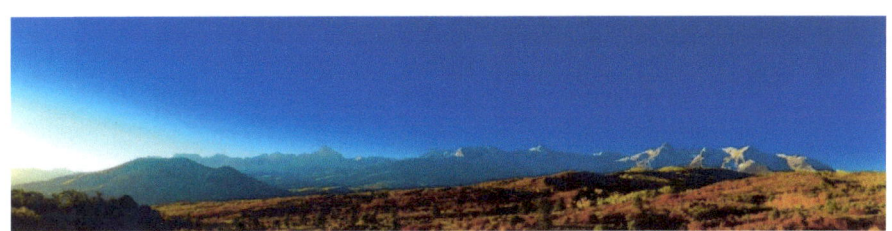

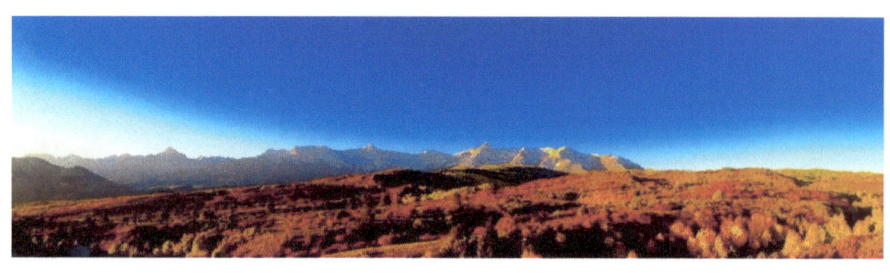

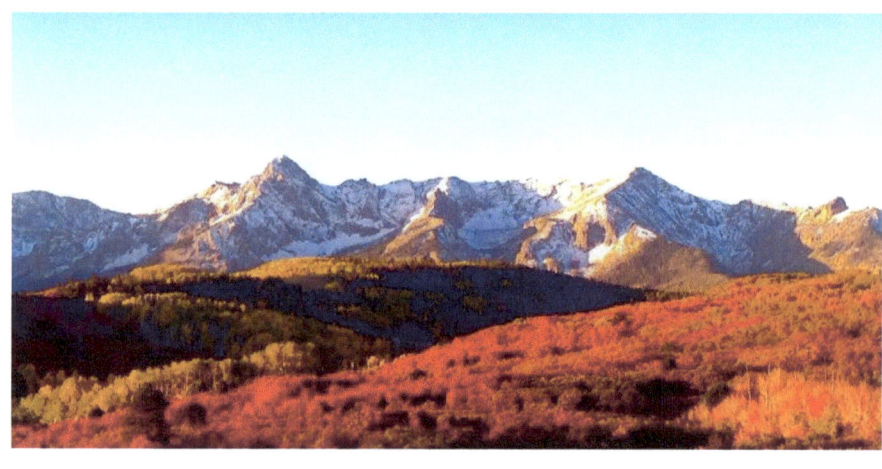

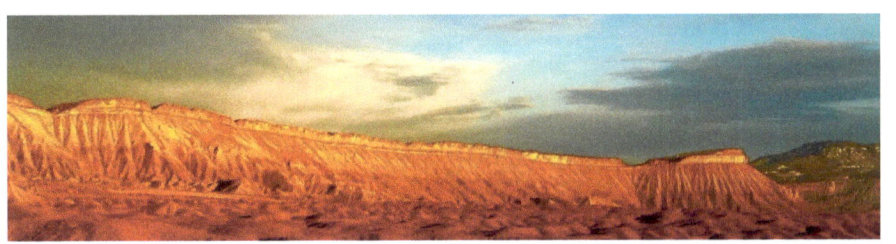

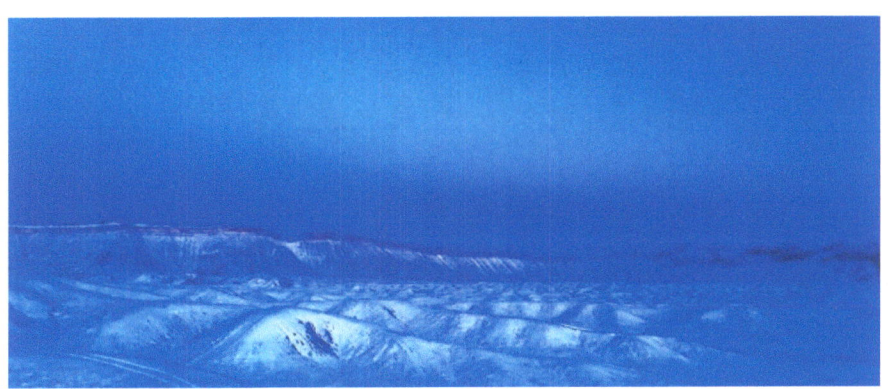

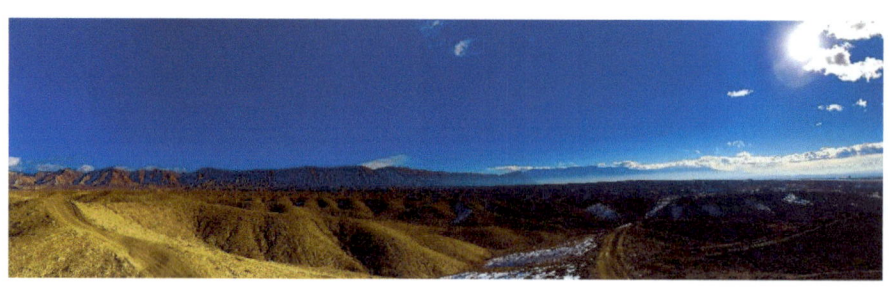

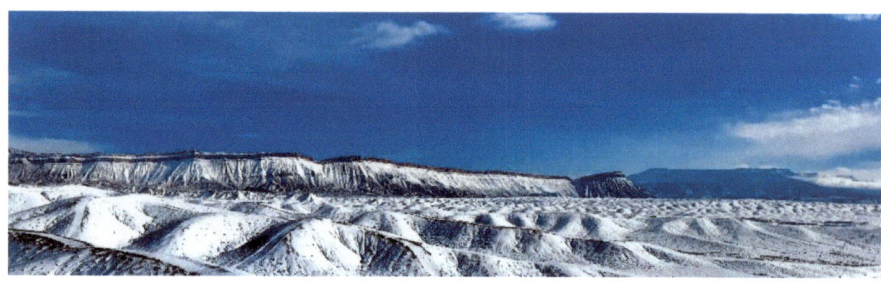

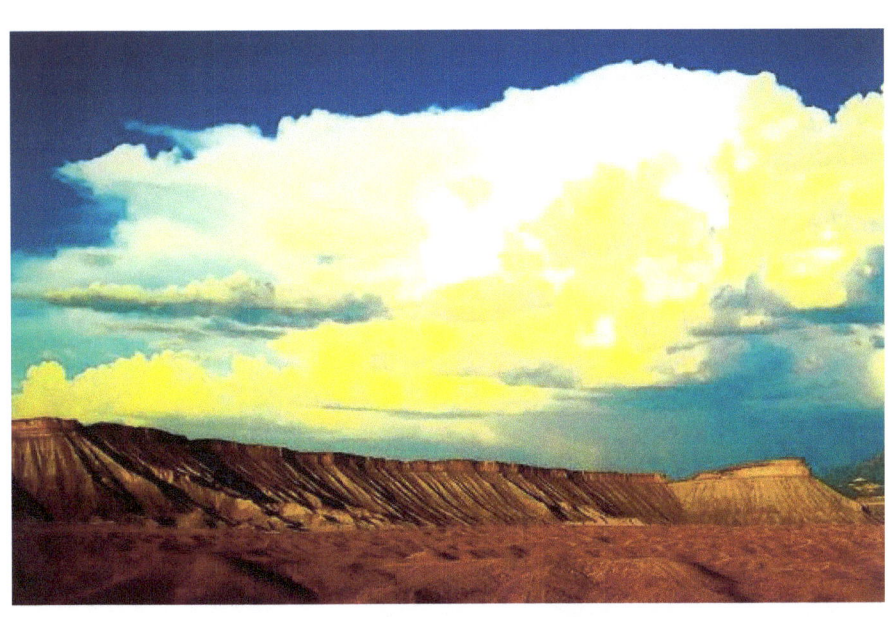
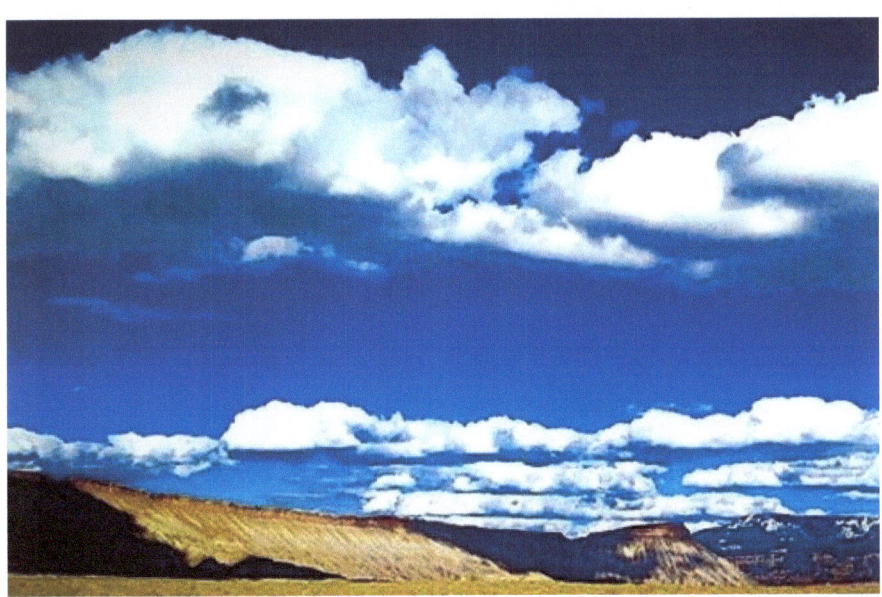

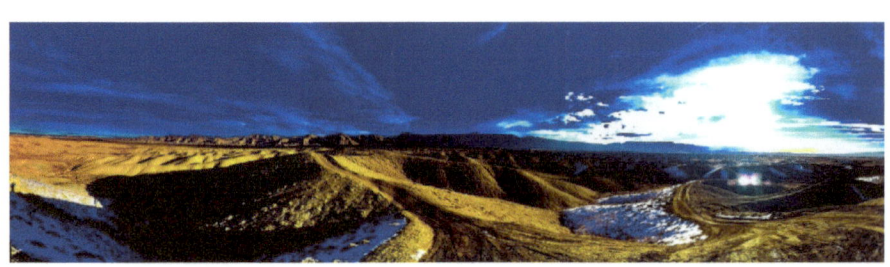

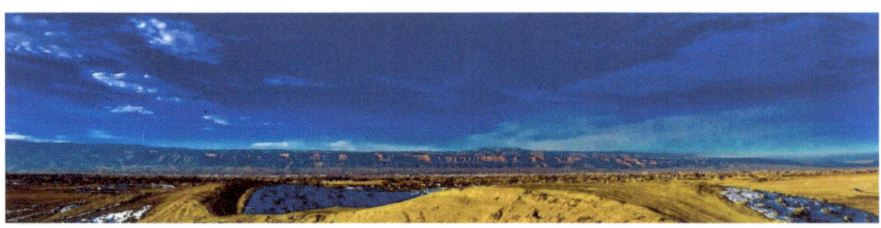

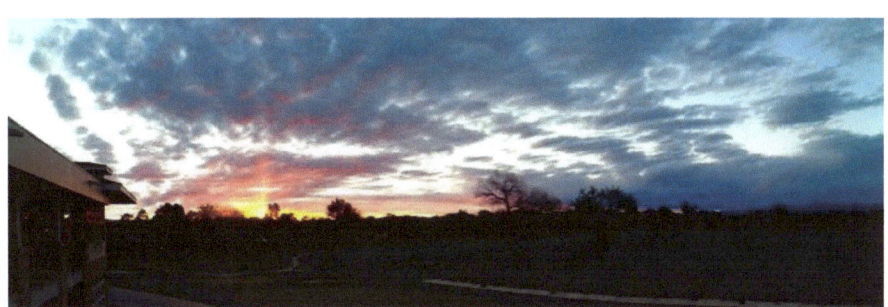

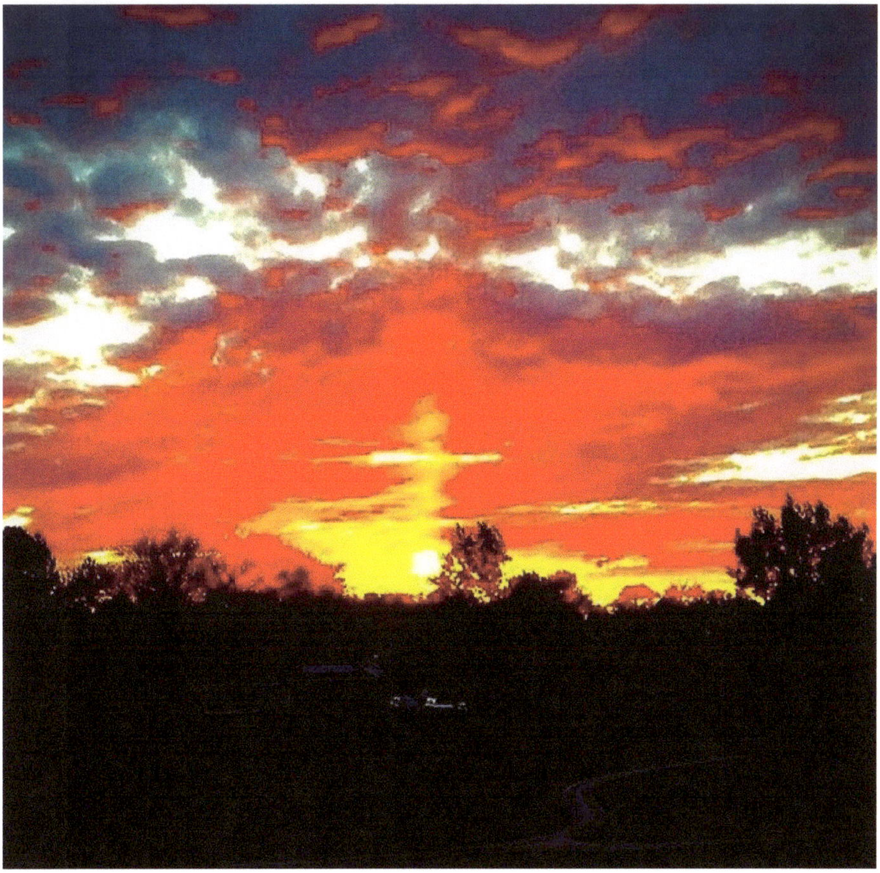

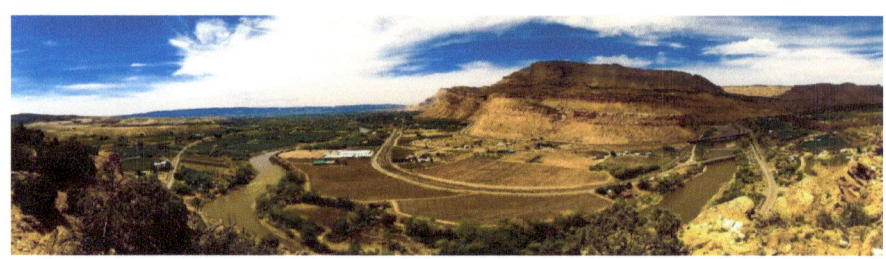

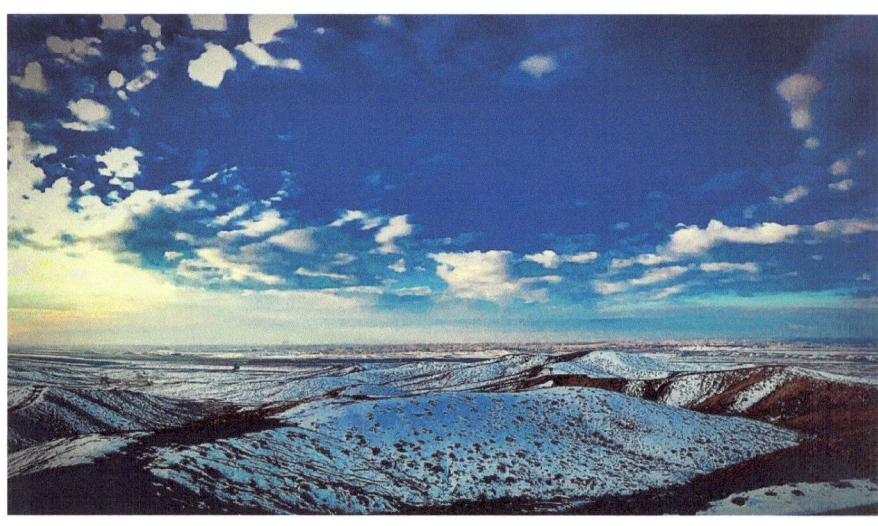

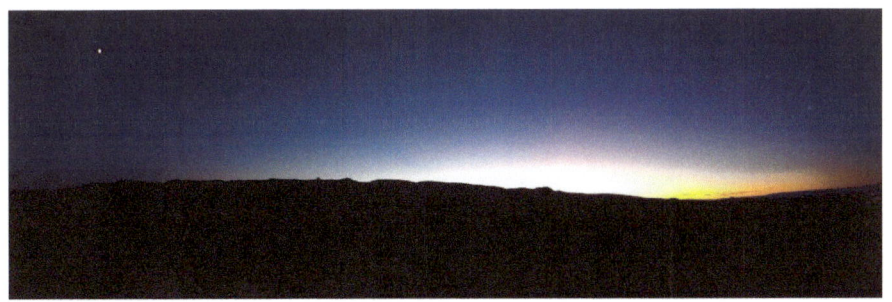
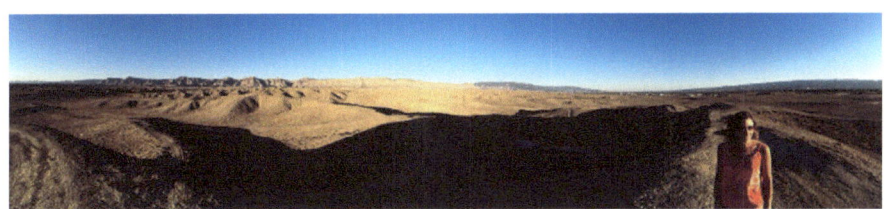

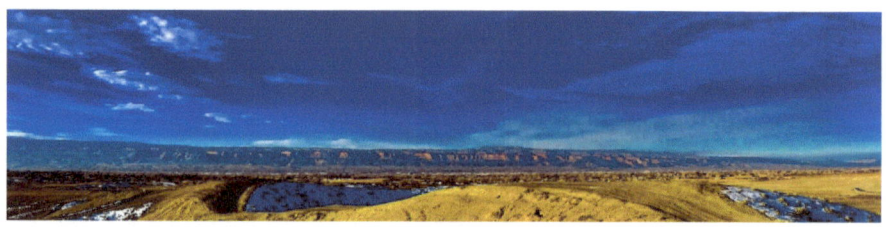

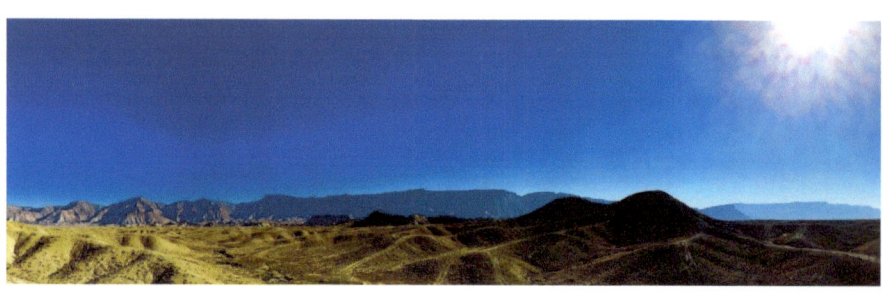

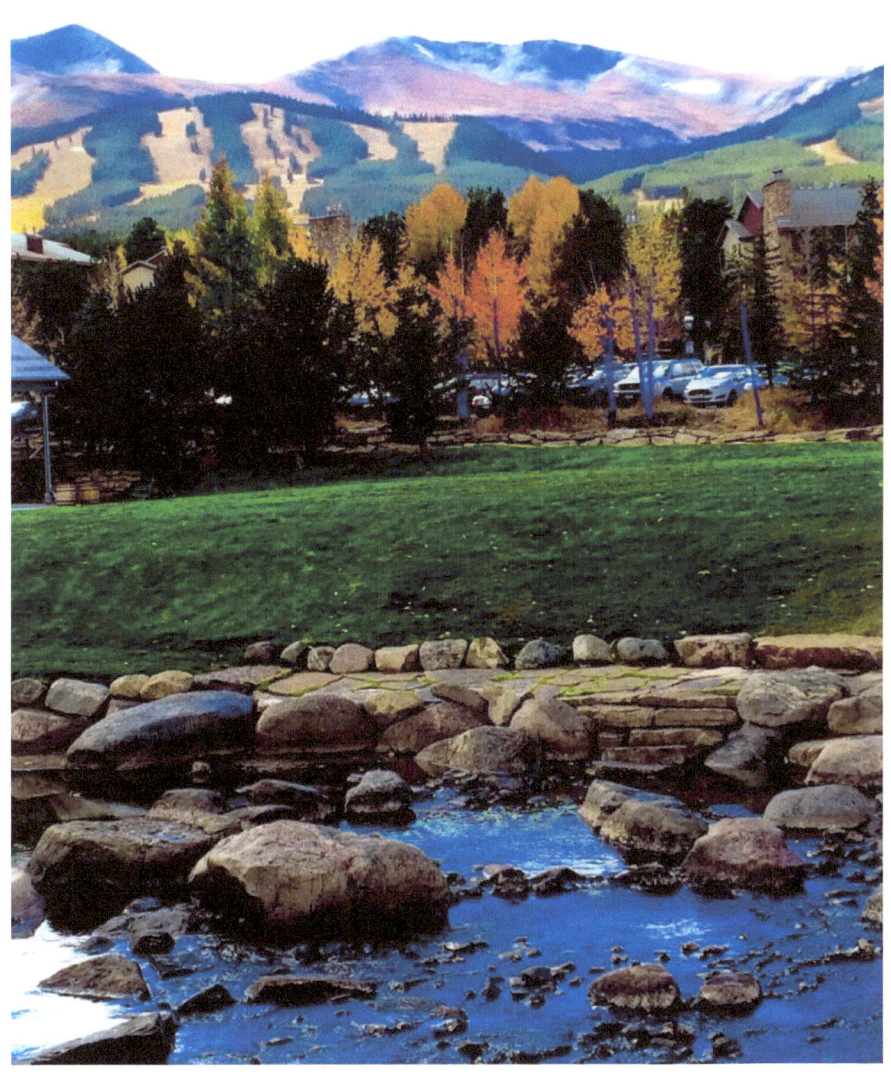

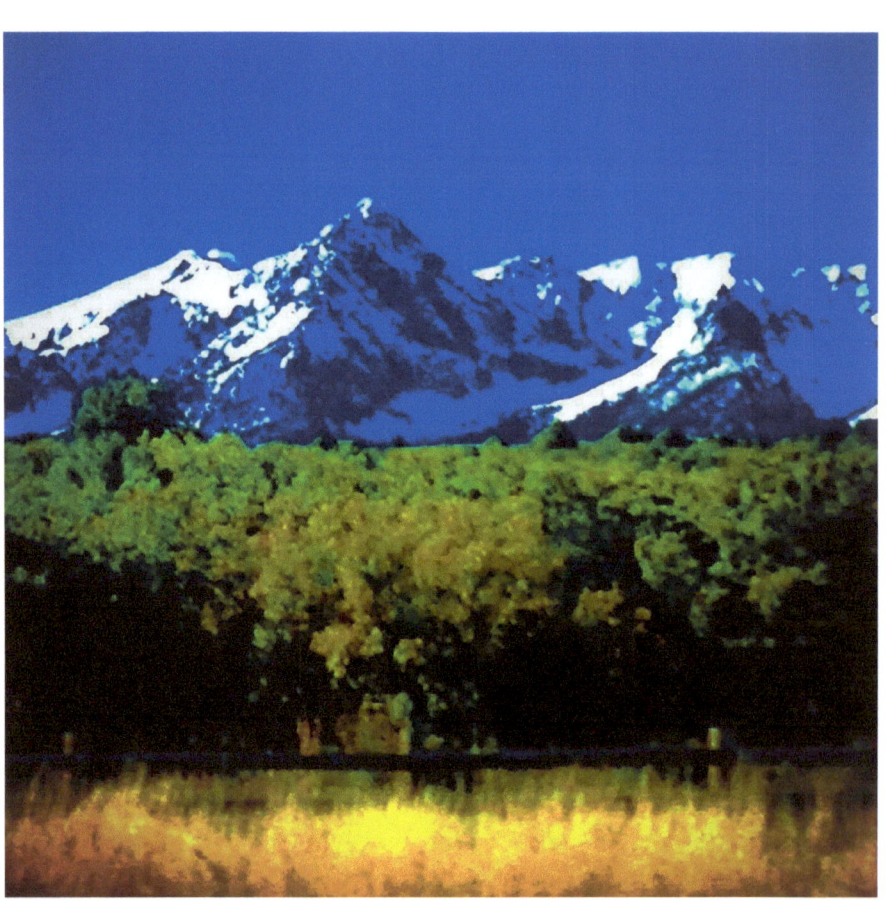

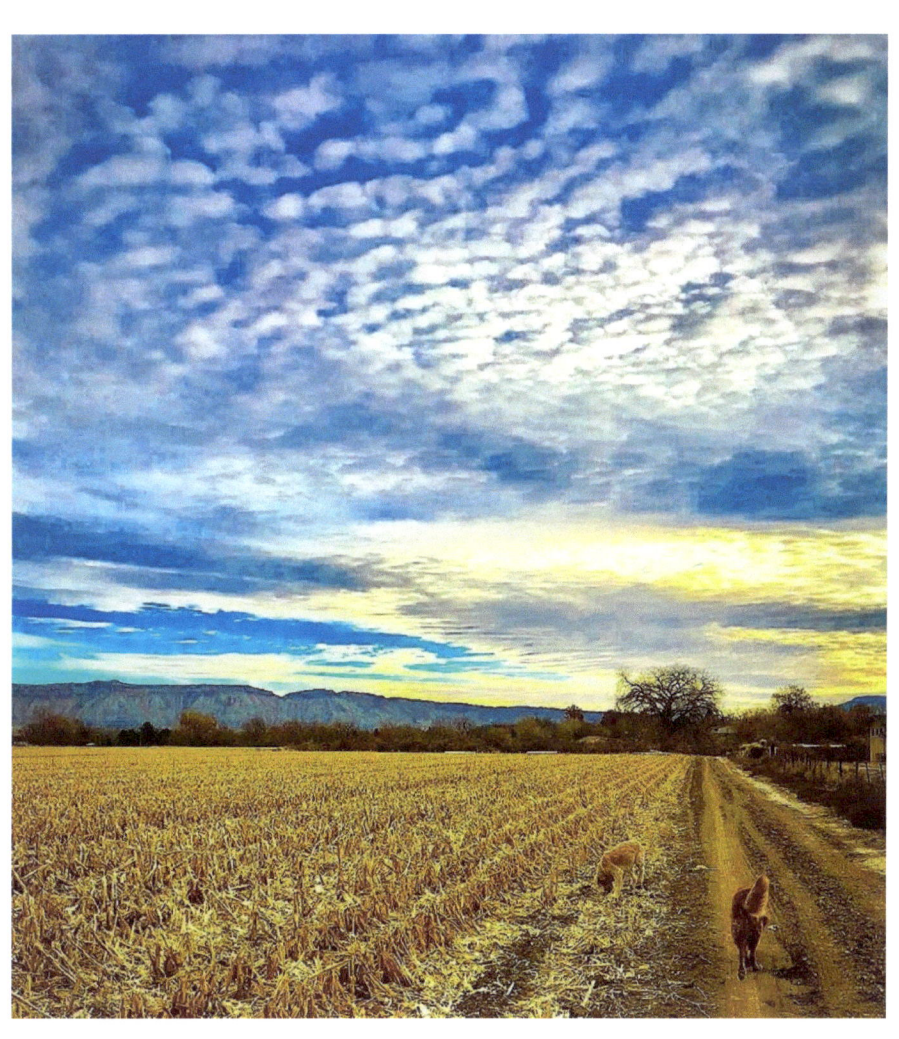

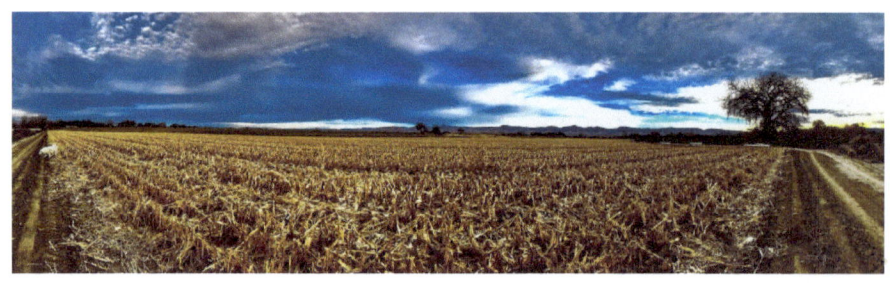

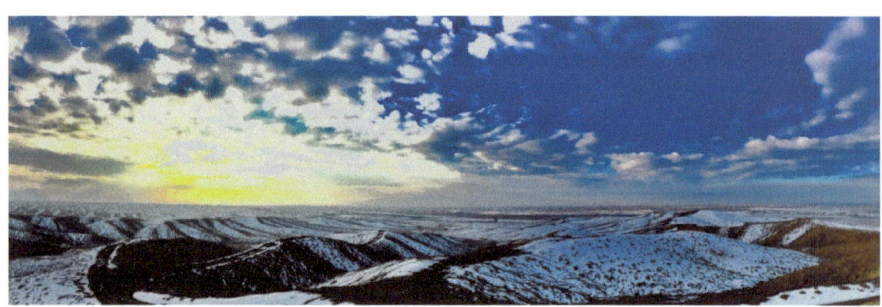

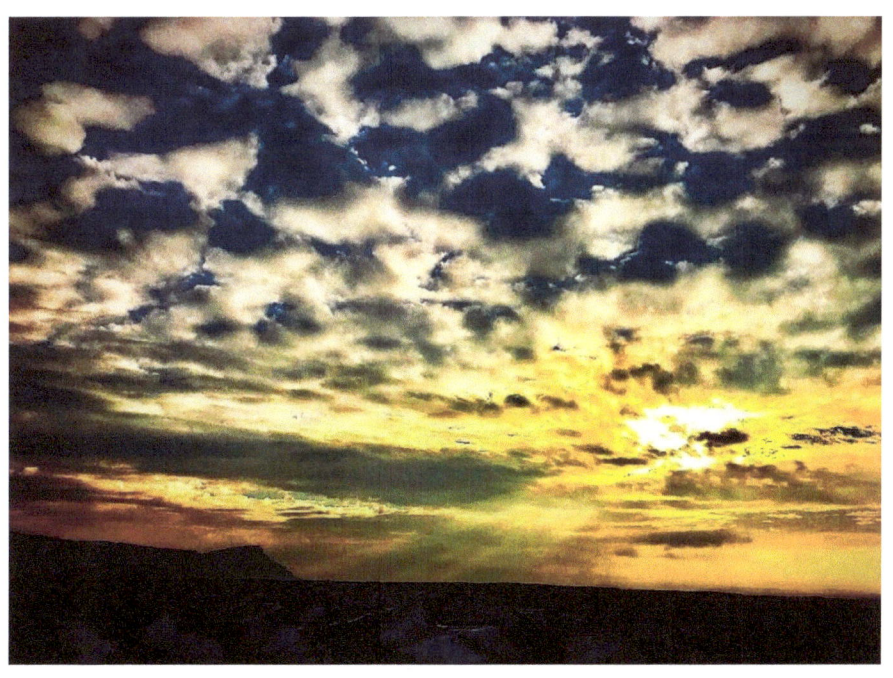

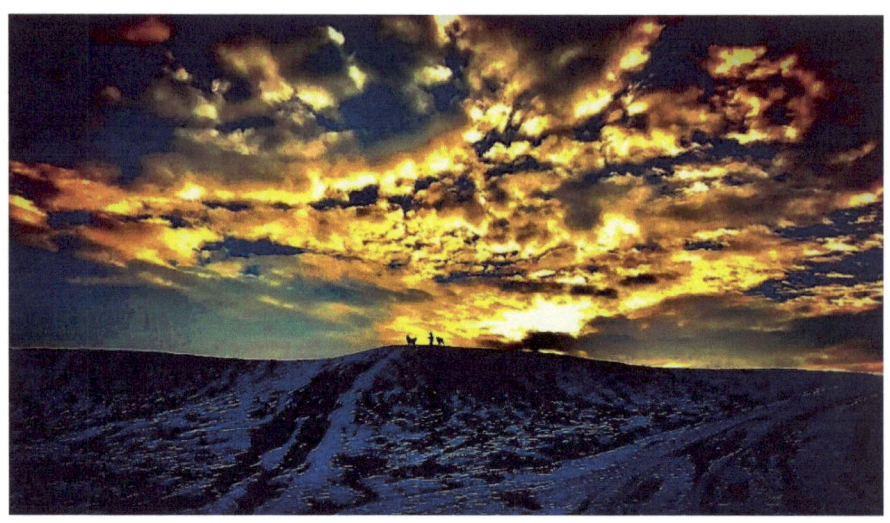

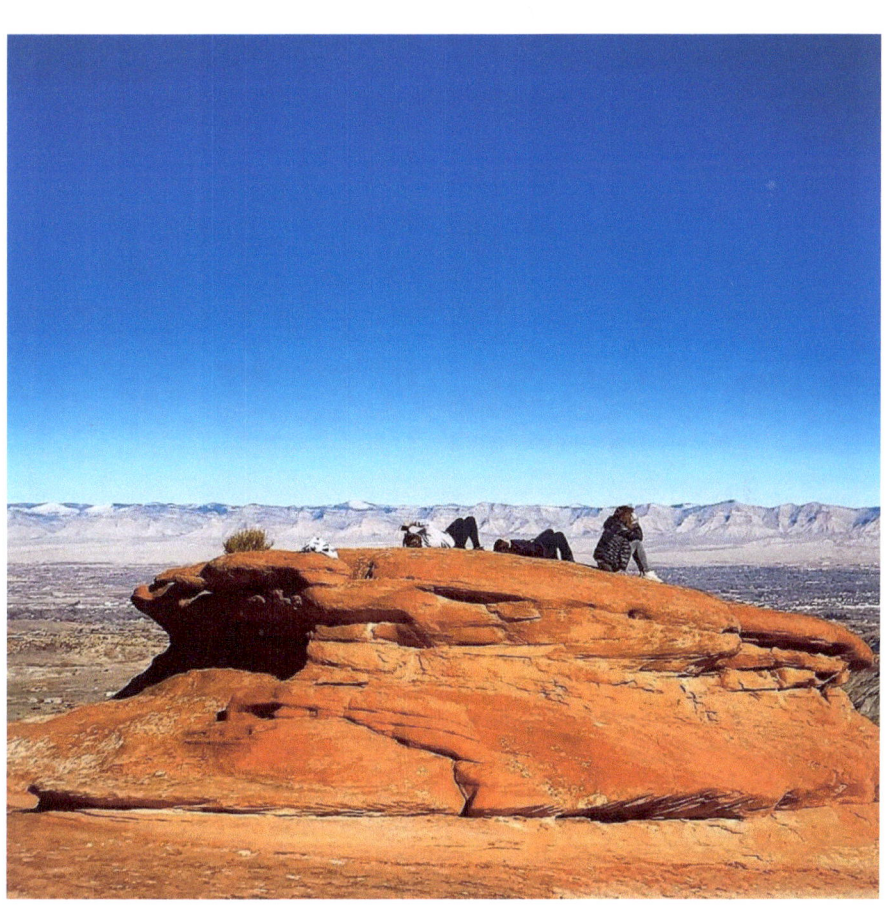

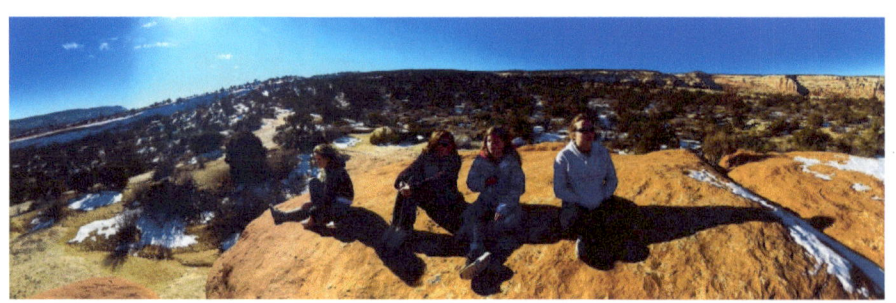

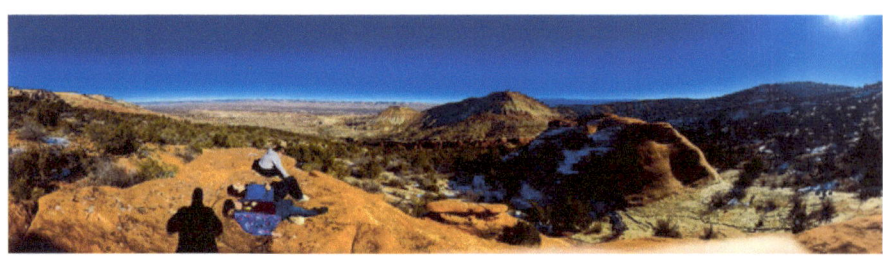

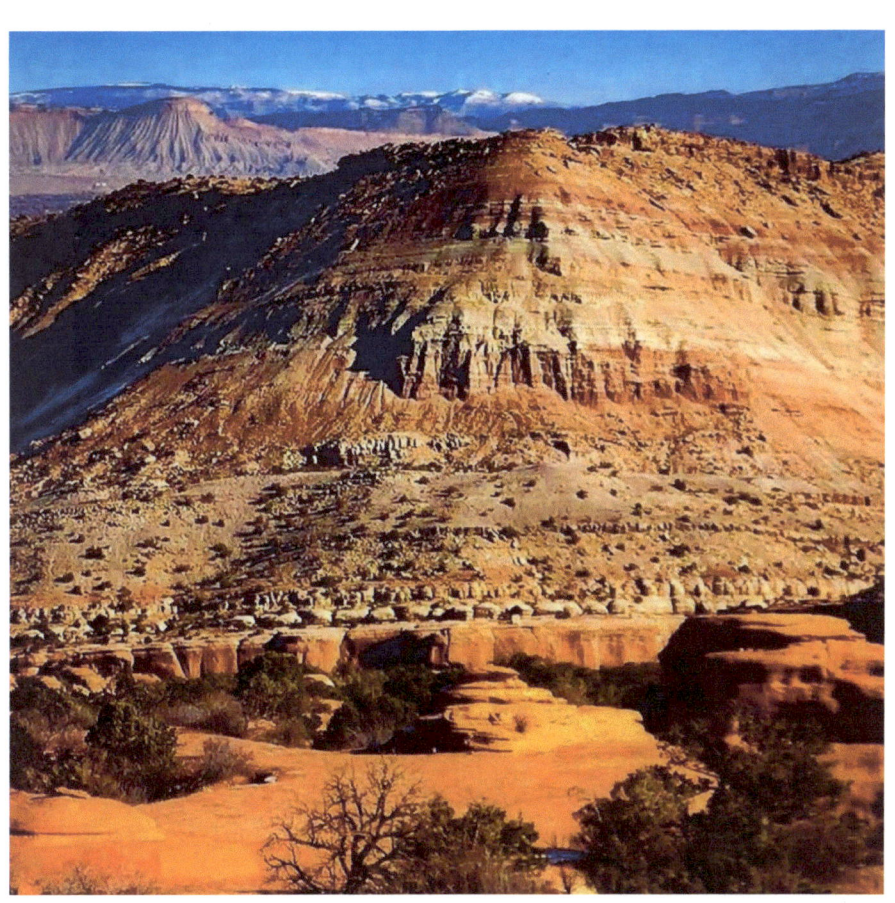

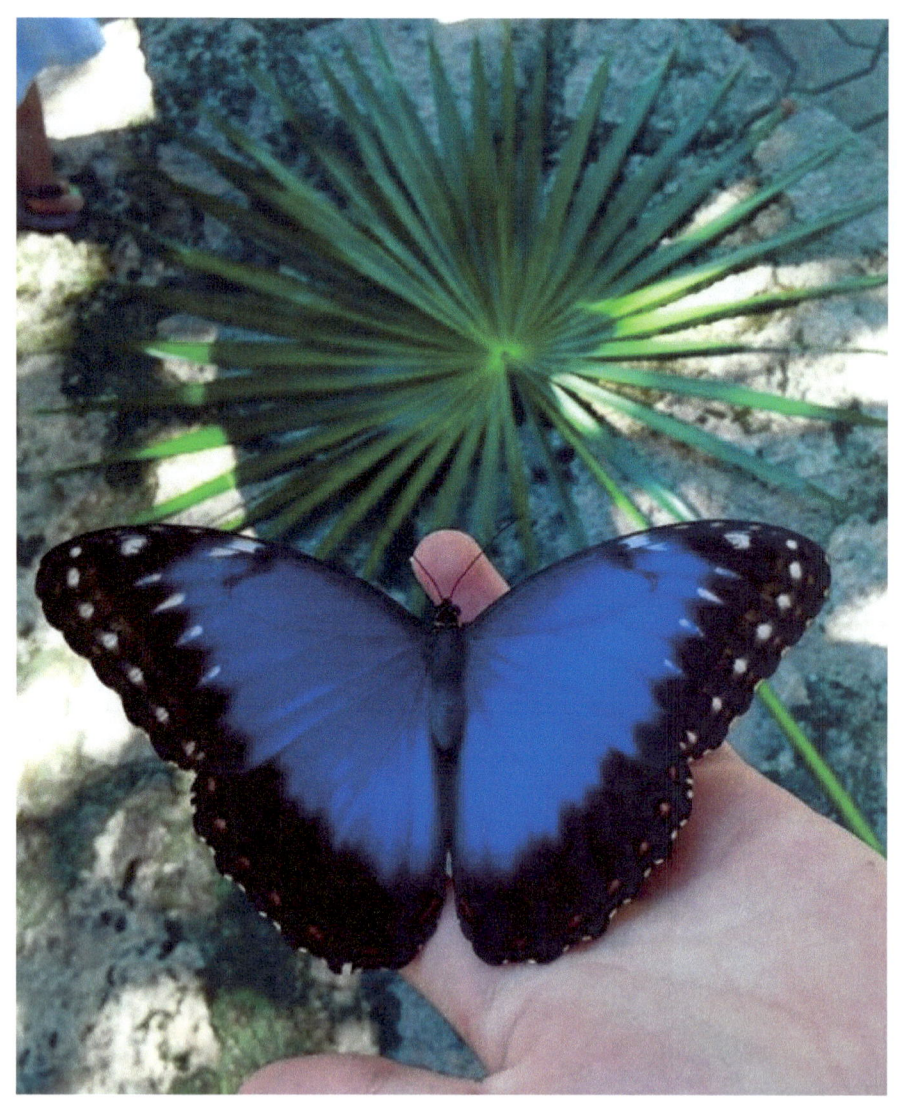

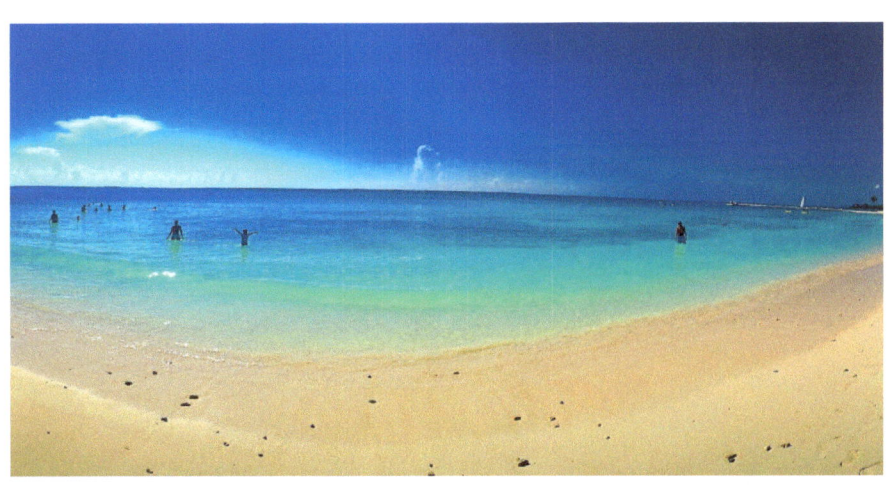

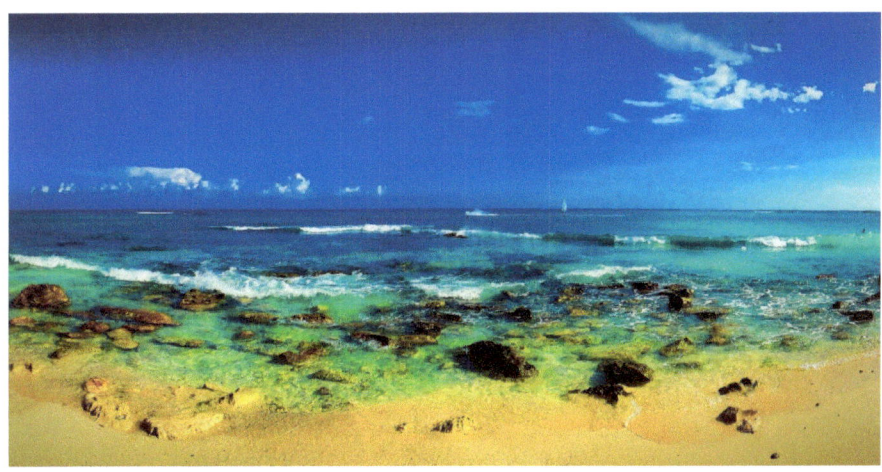

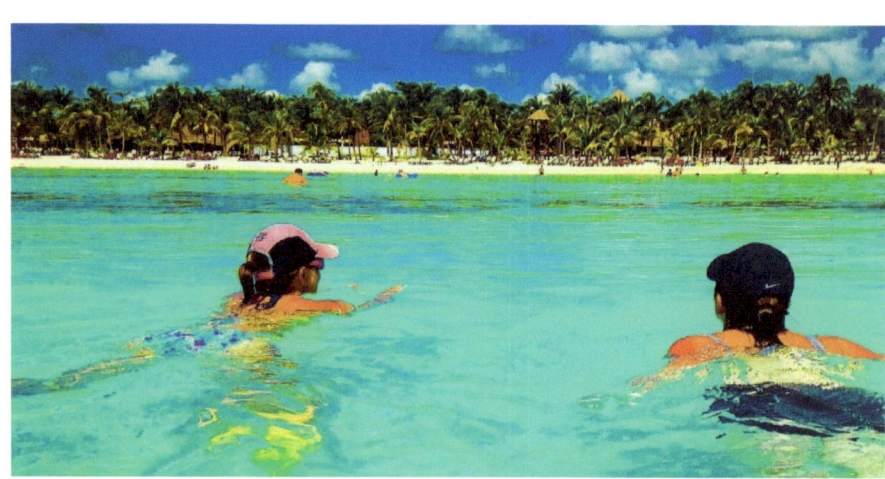
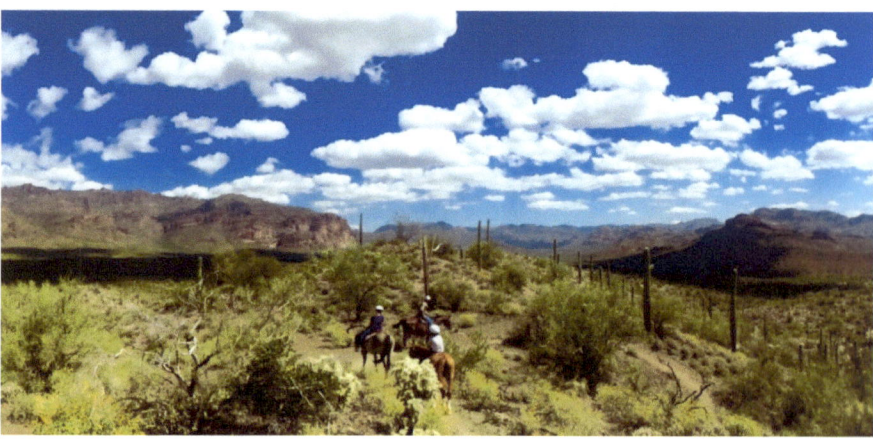

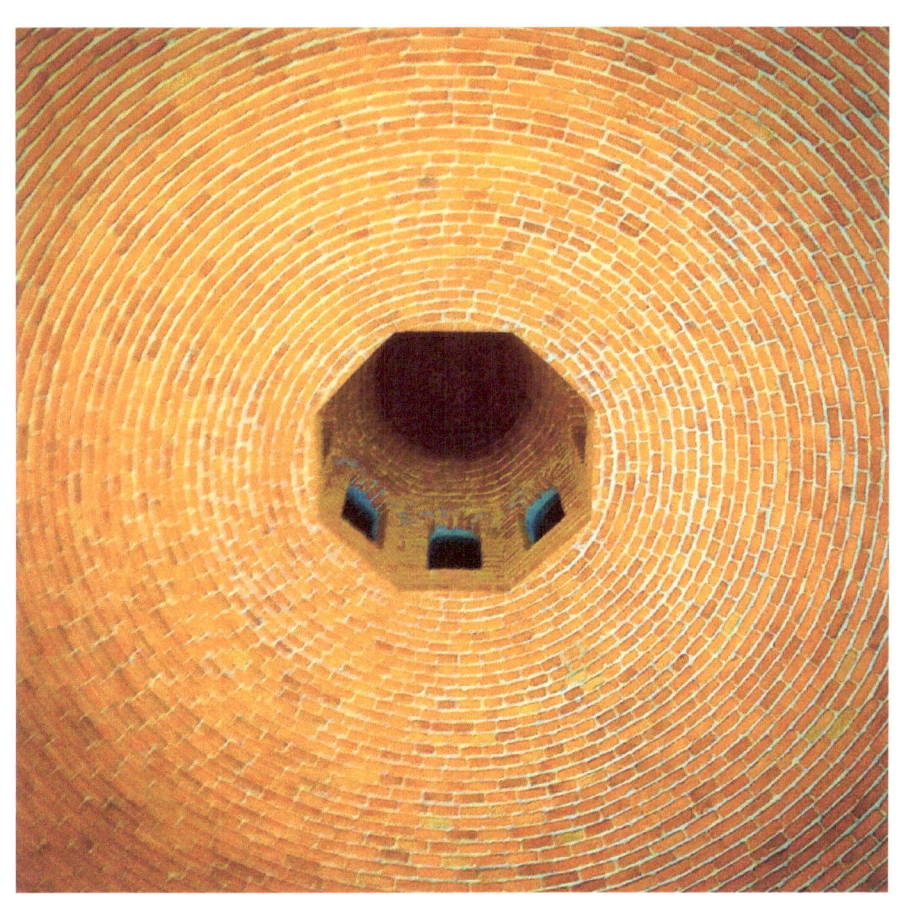

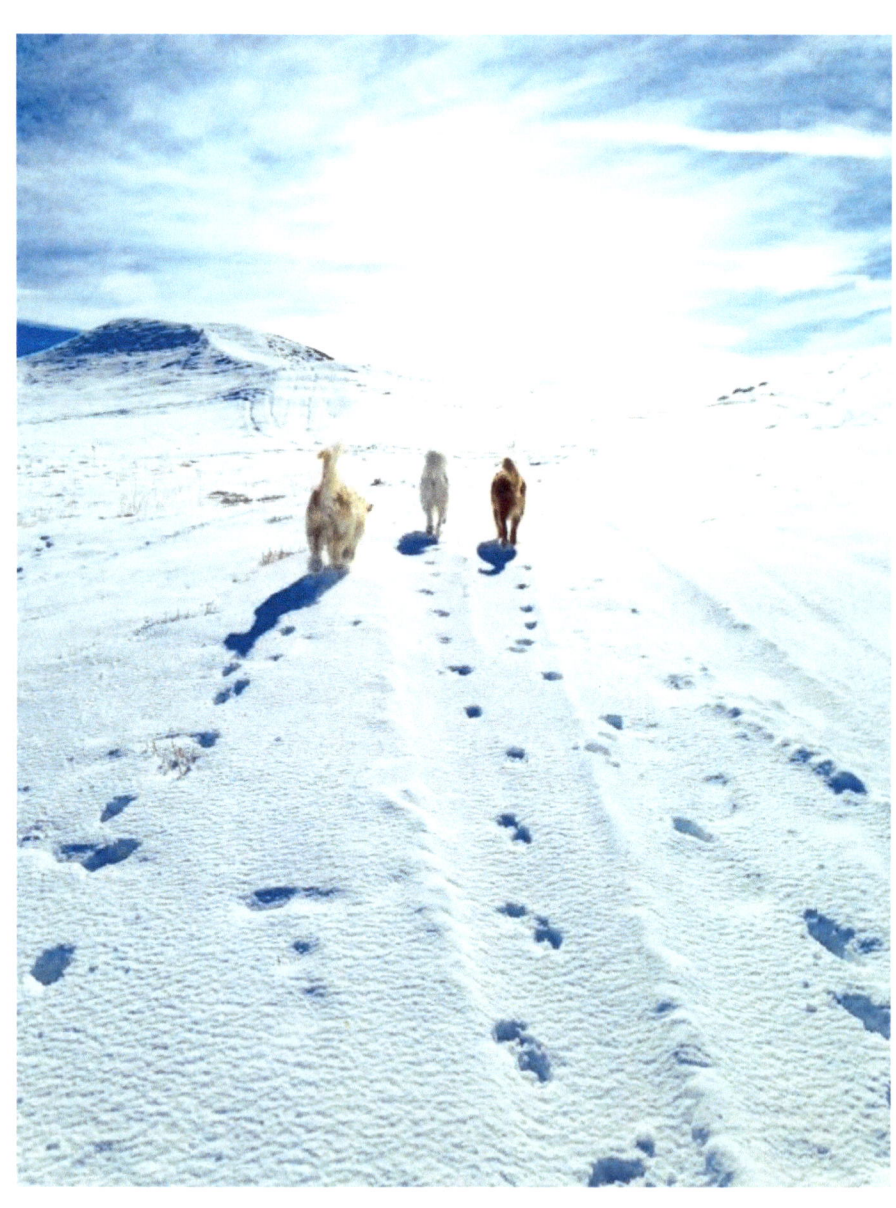

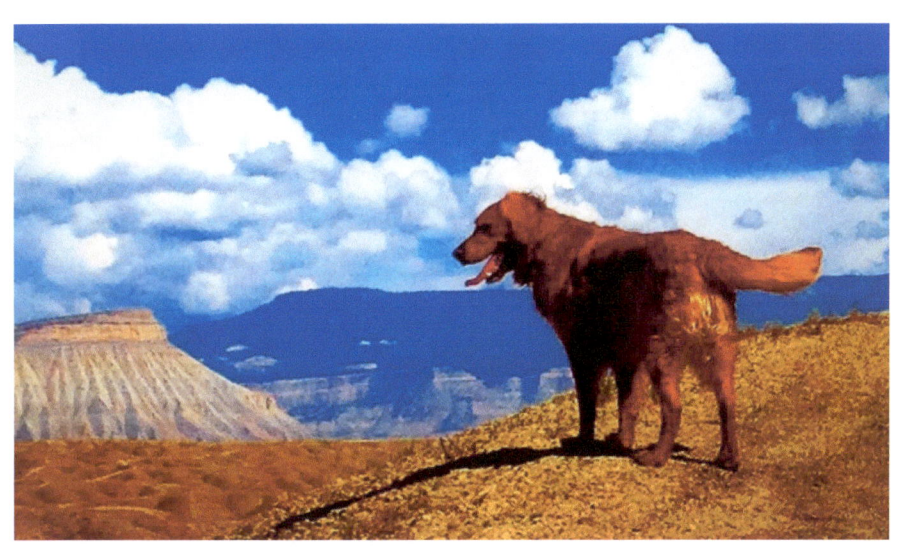

The End

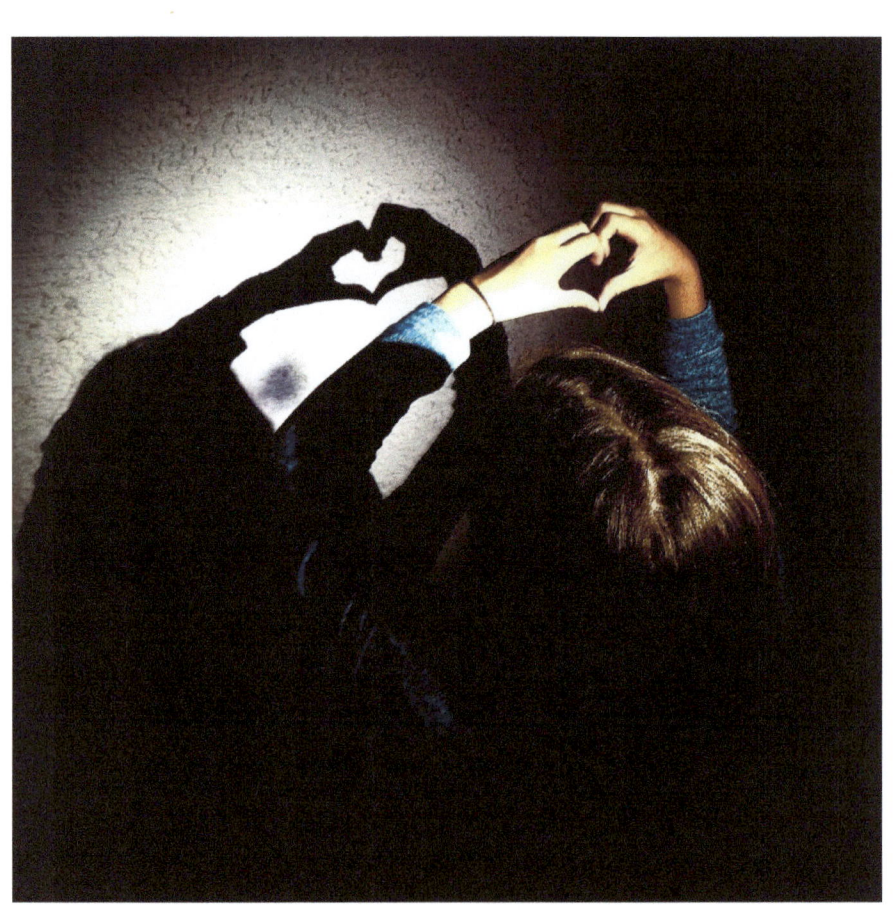

www.ingramcontent.com/pod-product-compliance
Lightning Source LLC
Chambersburg PA
CBHW040236220526
45473CB00001B/264